Dr. Lisa A. Reeves is an example of a quintessential modern woman who has achieved on a personal, professional and spiritual level. As her pastor, I am impressed with her spiritual development, her remarkable tenacity, her drive and uplifting perspective on life. This book is a must read for all persons who seek positive encouragement and perspective in facing the challenges of life.
— Rev. Dr. Nicholas Hood III, *Plymouth United Church of Christ.*

The character, Melissa, does an excellent job of demonstrating how scripture, belief and perseverance can get a person through life's challenges. Dr. Lisa A. Reeves' colorful style of detailing the journey of Melissa will intrigue you. Her examples of godly principles and relatable applications through Melissa's experiences will captivate you. The testimonies within this book serve as true testimony that God is real for all of us.
— Carnella Lewis, Senior Manager, *Johnson & Johnson (Neuroscience).*

The book, *Freedom, Peace and Joy: While in the Valley of Life*, is a powerful story of true faith in God. The book highlights one women's journey toward finding freedom and peace while in the dark, rough ridges in the deep valley of life.
Dr. Lisa A. Reeves breathes life into her principal character by providing emotionally scorching details and surprising revelations, while her character, Melissa, experiences one setback after another. Dr. Reeves engulfs the reader in unexpected lows and unimaginable highs, showcasing God's full spectrum of love and goodness! This is an excellent read for anyone ready to experience the promise of God. 5 Stars! ★★★★★
— Deborah J. Evans, CEO, *Walter Canyon Consulting*

Freedom, Peace & Joy
While in the Valley of Life

Dr. Lisa A. Reeves

PEGASUS BOOKS

Pegasus Books
8165 Valley Green Drive
Sacramento, CA 95823
www.pegasusbooks.net

First Edition: March 2020

Published in North America by Pegasus Books. For information, please contact Pegasus Books c/o Marcus McGee, 8165 Valley Green Drive, Sacramento, CA 95823

Library of Congress Cataloguing-In-Publication Data
Dr. Lisa A. Reeves
Freedom, Peace & Joy: While in the Valley of Life
Dr. Lisa A. Reeves – 1st ed
p. cm.
Library of Congress Control Number: 2010943502
ISBN – 978-1-941859-80-3
1. SELF-HELP / Personal Growth / Success. 2. RELIGION / Christian Living / Personal Growth. 3. FAMILY & RELATIONSHIPS / Life Stages / General. 4. SOCIAL SCIENCE / Ethnic Studies / American / African American Studies. 5. EDUCATION / Counseling / Academic Development.

10   9   8   7   6   5   4   3   2   1

Comments about *Freedom, Peace & Joy: While in the Valley of Life* and requests for additional copies, book club rates and author speaking appearances may be addressed to Dr. Lisa A. Reeves at lareeves1@sbcglobal.net, or you can send your comments and requests via e-mail to mmcgee@pegasusbooks.net.

Also available as an eBook from Internet retailers and from Pegasus Books

Printed in the United States of America

Dedication

Love is the Greatest Gift of All!

I dedicate this book to my husband, children, friends and church family. Thank you for your unconditional love.

To my husband, Julius: Words cannot express how grateful I am for your support. Throughout our marriage, you have been my greatest supporter. Thank you for advocating in all my endeavors. You are my rock and gift from God!

To my children, Lauren and Julian: Your inspiring words and technological assistance have meant the world to me. I am strengthened by your courage and boldness. It is my honor to be your mother!

To my nieces, Cinnamon, Ebony and Tracy: Your intelligence, courage and self-determination are amazing! God has a special plan for of each of you.

There are countless friends who have been major sources of support to me during this journey. I appreciate each of you. There are several individuals whose support I wish to highlight.

Deborah: It's been a blessing to have a friend with whom I can laugh and pray; you are such a leader.

Marvella: Your spiritual wisdom is limitless. I am a renewed person because of your example.

Carnella, my dearest friend in life: You have inspired me since childhood. I am motivated by your energy, your enthusiasm, and your execution of living your best life.

To the "Group": You are an amazing group of ladies, with class and kindness. I admire each of you.

To "Kindred," my book club sisters: Your intelligence, authenticity and grace are gifts from God. You have brought me so much laughter and joy.

To my Church Family: There is nothing like the Black Church. I appreciate your prayers and love. Thank you, prayer warrior sisters, for keeping my family uplifted and covered.

What a wonderful God that we serve. I praise and worship you!

Acknowledgments

To my parents, James O. and Sarah L. Banks: Thank you for your many sacrifices and always believing that I could accomplish my dreams. Your courage and self-determination to raise a family with love, joy, and hope have had a tremendous impact on my life. You were my biggest supporters and cheerleaders. I appreciate that you allowed me to be independent at an early age.

To my dear friend, Mignon: Thank you for walking this journey along with me and helping me. I could not have done this without you. You have been the best teacher. I appreciate our many conversations and the many lessons. You are my angel.

Katie McKnight: Thank you for showing a young girl, teenager, young lady, and woman unconditional love and for having a listening ear. You always made me feel like I could become somebody.

Finally, I thank Mrs. Walter Jean Jackson, for encouraging me to complete this book: Your words of wisdom to complete this assignment so that God could move me to the next assignment gave me peace to embrace my circumstances and appreciate the gift of time.

Dr. Lisa A. Reeves

While in the Valley of Life…

This book is an inspiration for getting through life's valley with self-determination, faith, and joy and ultimately reaching one's pinnacle achievements and goals. In this story, our writer Dr. Reeves, shows how Melissa maintains her vision, hope and faith as she strives to climb out of the valley to reach her mountain top.

Through the academic lens of Black Feminist Thought, Womanism, Self-Determination, and Spirituality, Dr. Reeves includes relevant scriptures to uplift and guide you through the difficult times of life, helping you to find stability and fulfillment.

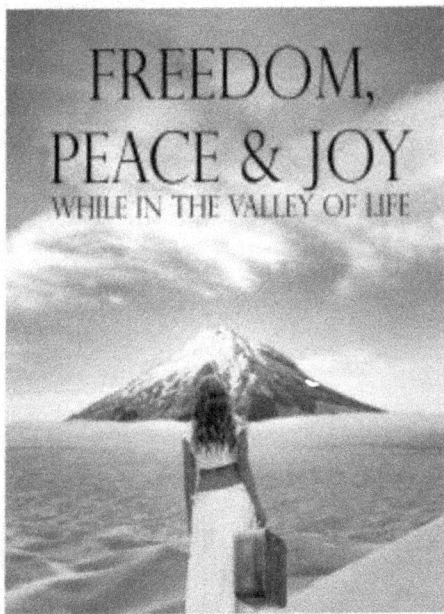

FREEDOM,
PEACE & JOY
WHILE IN THE VALLEY OF LIFE

Table of Contents

Now the Lord is the Spirit, and where the Spirit of the Lord is, there is freedom. — Corinthians 2 3:17

Come quickly, Lord and answer me, for my strength is fading. Don't turn away from me, or I will join those who are descending to the grave — Psalm 143:7

Then he told them many things in parables, saying: "A farmer went out to sow his seed — Matthew 13:3

You are coming to Christ, who is the living cornerstone of God's temple. He was rejected by people, but he was chosen by God for great honor —1 Peter 2:4

Everything on earth has its own time and its own season — Ecclesiastes 3:1

For we are his workmanship, created in Christ Jesus for good works, which God prepared beforehand, that we should walk in them. — Ephesians 2:10

This shall be the sign to you from the LORD, that the LORD will do this thing that He has spoken — Isaiah 38:7

For I reckon that the sufferings of this present time [are] not worthy [to be compared] with the glory which shall be revealed in us. — Romans 8:18

So do not fear, for I am with you; do not be dismayed, for I am your God. I will strengthen you and help you; I will uphold you with my righteous right hand. — Isaiah 41:10

Whatever you do, work heartily, as for the Lord and not for men. — Colossians 3:23

As for man, his days are like grass; As a flower of the field, so he flourishes. When the wind has passed over it, it is no more, And, its place acknowledges it no longer. — Psalms 103: 15-16

i

Your beginnings will seem humble, so prosperous will your future be. — Job 8:7
I am the vine, and you are branches. Those who remain in me, and I in them, will bear much fruit; for you can do nothing without me.— John 15:5
I have no one else like him who genuinely cares about your welfare. — Philippians 2:20
My dear friends, we are now God's children, but it is not yet clear what we shall become. But we know that when Christ appears, we shall be like him, because we shall see him as he really is. — 1 John 3:2
He restoreth my soul; He leadeth me in the paths of righteousness for His name's sake. — 1 Psalms 23:3

Freedom, Peace and Joy

A story of black self-determination, told through the academic lens of Spirituality, Black Feminist Thought and Womanism.

Black Self-Determination – An intrinsic motive of Black folks to achieve a goal. Historically, the Black Church provided a place for praise, hope, strength, and support. It is a place where self-determination was encouraged. V.P. Franklin (1992) notes that Black Americans have a lineage of self-determination based on historic experiences of enduring slavery, living in oppressive climates, and migrating from their homes in the south to acquire better living conditions in the north. This self-determination to move across the country with a hope and desire to achieve a better life was an example of hope and faith.

Spirituality – Spirituality holds different meanings, whether it is connected to traditional religious view or it is experienced through music, meditation or other forms of expression. It evokes a sense of wholeness connectedness-at-work and deeper values (Milliman, J., Czaplewski, A., & Ferguson, J. 2003).

Black Feminist Thought (BFT) – This is a social theory developed by Patricia Hills-Collins, in which she suggested that class oppression, sexism and racism are inextricably linked. For black women, these multiple identities were characteristics that were being used to discriminate against them. This oppression results from any unjust situation in which, systematically and over a long timespan, one group denies another group access to the resources of society (Collins, 2002). BFT allows the stories and voices of those black women who are most affected to be spoken and heard.

Womanism – Alice Walker coined the term womanism in the late 1970's and early 1980's. The term was created for

Black women to express themselves and their beliefs separate and apart from White Feminism, with a spiritual view. This is an expression, which allowed black women to tell their stories from their point of view, and they would be at the center of their experience (Harris, 2010).

Preface

Now the Lord is the Spirit, and where the Spirit of the Lord is, there is freedom. — **2 Corinthians 3:17**

Finding freedom, peace, and joy while in the valley of life...

She was in a valley. Melissa had entered a phase in her life where she was experiencing a tremendous amount of change, disappointment and uncertainty. Life was out of her control.

Using the analogy of a symphony concert, her orchestrated suburban life was out of sync. Strings were out-of- tune and were popping off her musical instrument in many different lengths and directions. Stroke after stroke, it seemed, that life's touch impacted not just one item, but many strings were broken or were just out-of-sync instead.

There were multiple issues. The melody that she once played no longer had harmony. Discouraged and distraught after all the practice, she had hoped to restructure the symphony to compose the right tune and melody, which currently sounded like a culmination of sabotage. What she yearned for most was stability, answers and fulfillment.

She wanted to resume a position of knowing what to expect and having some feeling of control over her destiny. She believed that having a feeling of knowing would bring a sense of stability and fulfillment. More than anything, she wanted to be back in a position of certainty, for she believed it would give her a feeling of wholeness. However, ultimately, she knew that to be in a state of certainty meant she was not fully trusting God.

Melissa wanted to live a life in the realm of what God created her to be. She wanted to live her life in the purpose of what God had destined for her. She knew to live her life in God's will meant she would have to accept the mysteries of life, which contradicted having complete control. She would not always have the answers.

This way of living was in opposition to what she desired, which was to be in control. What she would learn is that when she relinquished control and surrendered to God, ultimately, she would attain freedom peace and joy.

Introduction

In the Valley When It's Dark and You Cannot See

Even though I walk through the darkest valley, I will fear no evil, for you are with me; your rod and your staff, they comfort me — **Psalm 23:4**

Two years earlier, Melissa had entered her valley and had no idea what it would entail to get out. Her valley was one of many current tribulations. Her valley would soon be defined as "the loss of her job, the inability to quickly obtain another job, the deaths of several close family members, numerous instances of illnesses within the family, loss of friendships, changes in her weight, and rejections from several potential jobs."

She thought some people, while in the valley, attempted to ignore the issues. Others assume the victim role and tirelessly complain, while others find themselves drowning in depression or finding their comfort in food. Melissa wanted to be one who learned from her valley and heard God.

She recognized the valley was a place we all must enter, and she knew she needed to learn to survive and thrive while in the valley. She found that the valley was the place in which she would share her deepest thoughts, concerns and worries with her Heavenly Father. Although it was a time that her faith would be challenged, it was also a time that her faith would be fueled.

The Descent

Come quickly, Lord and answer me, for my strength is fading. Don't turn away from me, or I will join those who are descending to the grave. — **Psalm 143:7**

Rolling down an avalanche—sometimes falling faster than she imagined possible, and certainly rendered her more out of control than she wanted, Melissa entered her valley quickly.

When she wasn't rolling out of control into her valley, she rolled down the avalanche in slow motion, watching each bump jerk her back and forth. What she didn't realize was that she was entering a dark place where she would occupy the space for a period over two and half years.

During her valley moments, her faith would be shaken, tested and tried. This valley journey was paradoxical, for at the same time, she underwent low moments, though she also experienced incredibly high peaks.

There were peak moments, where she would receive manna for each day, but she would just have to reach out and grab it. While traveling in the valley at her weakest point, she would feel the arms of God coddling her, carrying her during the most difficult times, and providing nuggets of encouragement to sustain her enough to get her through to another day.

She would have to grow strong, learn to adapt in her valley, reach for the manna and still have a dream—even though there were days that she could barely get out of the bed and start her day. On the many days when she did not want to get out of bed and face the uncertainty of what was to come, she relied on scripture to strengthen her. She learned to strengthen her spirit and feed her mind to grab the manna that was provided for that particular day.

She was raised in the church and knew God's word said that there would be *trials and tribulations and to consider it pure joy* — **James 1:2.** But How? She knew things would go wrong in life and there would be uncomfortable situations. She thought, you must remember that *your Heavenly Father is with you, even when it does not appear so*. It is the Lord who goes before you. He will be with you; he will not fail you or forsake you. She would hold onto *Do not fear or be dismayed* — **Deuteronomy 31:8.**

She knew that life presented valley moments of disappointments, discouragement and sadness. No one was exempt from it. One's valley could be defined in many ways. It involves those actions that are not controllable. Valley moments cause someone *not to have* peace or joy.

They are the times that cause a person to question even the *existence and the will of God*. One's sleep is disrupted, and that person is repeatedly haunted with the question about what is going on? During that time, she knew she had to dig deeply to tap into her reservoir of faith and strength.

She knew she had to deal with the situation by embracing it, acknowledging the loss, feeling the pain, confronting the disappointment, yet she knew she was not alone—that God comforts us in all our troubles so that we can comfort others. She knew, from the experiences of hurt, that she would be able to give others the same comfort God had given her. — 2 Corinthians 1:4.

She continually refocused and realized that she must remember that no one escapes suffering. We all face moments of uncertainty. She was not alone—not even Jesus was spared. The valley moments are a testing of one's faith.

It is not the end of someone's story, but rather it strengthens and enriches that narrative. It is a process that all humans must experience. Remember, Jesus suffered. He begged God with loud crying and tears to save him. He truly worshiped God, and *God listened to his prayers*. — **Hebrews 5:7.** He went through trials, and in time, he rose, and so would she. The Holy Spirit strengthened her resolve to continue to worship God during these trials.

In the valley, when it's dark, when someone has lost hope and has a sad heart, one must remember that *God cannot lie* — **Hebrews 6:18.** His promises and vows are two things that can never be changed. No matter how dark someone's situation may be, how big the loss, how humiliating the situation, how wrong is the action, if a person is able to hold on to this tidbit of knowledge and have faith, God's promises and vows are true.

There is hope while in the valley. God will be there. His promises should greatly encourage us to *take hold of the hope that is right in front us* — **Hebrews 6:18.**

Chapter 1

Walking in the Valley

Then he told them many things in parables, saying: "A farmer went out to sow his seed..." — Matthew 13:3

52... A Mid-Life Crisis...

For most of her life, she had done things in a compliant and respectful manner. She lived a life where she didn't rock the boat, but rather went in the direction of the waves. Yet she had come to a time when she knew things would be different. She would have to make bold decisions, and she would have to do some drastic things.

She had to be audacious and courageous and step out of her comfort zone. There would have to be a shift in her thinking and actions, a shift that was beyond her norm.

Abruptly, at age 52, her life had been disrupted. What she thought she had control over—her job, her children, her family relationships, friendships, and even weight—quickly unraveled before her eyes. Her life had been neatly organized, controlled, packaged, strategically planned, and well-executed.

However, it was no longer so well-ordered. Suddenly, her life was turned upside down! Instantly, all the pieces were being dismantled! What she knew and came to expect would radically shift.

Within one month after her mother's death, she learned her job would be eliminated. Then a few days later, her son decided to drop out of college to pursue a business venture. She was unspeakably saddened by the death of her mother and was grieving. Despite her grieving and loss, there was more anguish and concern for her son and herself.

Although it was not the same sort of loss, nevertheless it increased her grief and pain. She was walking in a valley, and the valley moments grew deeper.

Within a year, there was more loss. Her mother-in-law died and a month after, unexpectedly her sister drowned. If all these events were not bad enough, her eldest sister became gravely ill and had become incapacitated. Her brothers were battling life issues due to consequences from previous substance abuse. Her life was in a state of uncertainty and chaos. She felt as if she was drowning in a deep dark pool of uncertainty.

Her world had shifted drastically, rapidly—dreams and people were dying. She no longer had control over her life she previously had. She did not know what was going on, and she did not know what to call it. Ordinarily, she would not have labeled her situation to be a "mid-life crisis," since she never thought the term could be applied to her.

She associated the term with older men, who "wanted to get their groove back," or it was a denial of the inevitable aging of a male. It was a stage she never considered might be applied to anyone who looked like her.

Yet as she analyzed the recent series of events in her life and her age, she thought the series of events at her age certainly might qualify as a mid-life crisis. She turned 53, an age considered to be the middle-point of a life fully lived. And the events in her life were certainly a crisis!

The events were mini crises that could not be ignored. The incidents were problematic, and there was no longer a semblance of normalcy in her life. She was in a valley, filled with many potholes and ditches, with a severe storm hovering overhead. She was discouraged, distraught, and she felt discombobulated.

The Cracks of Life

As she reflected on her circumstances, she realized there had been warning signs and portents for the oncoming storm.

There were rumblings in her thoughts, an uneasiness in her spirit and an unsettling feeling from which she could not flee or avoid her restlessness.

Usually, she was intuitive and quick to pick up on things, but she had ignored all the signs. Reflecting on recent examples of distressing events, she had heard troubling details from her siblings about her mother's health, while she knew the climate on her job had shifted, and her son had earlier announced he desired to pursue his passions and dreams.

Were these the signals of the shift? Absolutely! Were they the warnings of the tide to come? Yes, but she had ignored the signs. Yes, the stabilizing factors in her life were disappearing or dying. She never imagined it possible, but the evidence was there.

She knew intuitively that a change was coming. Her spirit and soul were restless, and there had been many times where she felt the uneasiness. Her life had changed, but she had chosen to overlook the signs and facts.

The organized, neatly packed box of her life had burst from the bottom. It collapsed right through her hands, right before her eyes, with several items shattered and fallen on the ground.

Her previous life, in contrast, was one that kept her overly occupied. She believed all the activities that occupied her would bring the joy and happiness she always desired. Yet internally she knew the activities were occupying space and time. Some of the activities were a façade of happiness.

It was inevitable that her life would make a shift due to her antsy thoughts, boredom and overactive personality. But she never imagined the change would be such a jolting, seismic shift. Abruptly, her daily routine came to a halt.

She no longer woke up at the crack of dawn to workout, rush to work, parent her children, go to classes, make the next volunteer organization meeting, prepare dinner, talk with her husband, read a book and then go to sleep.

She had time to contemplate her inner thoughts as she completed her PhD studies and searched for her next position or endeavor. The disruption caused her to sit quietly, reflecting on, questioning things, including her faith, while waiting for her next assignment. She had time *to hear God*, since several things that blocked her listening to God's messages had been removed from her life.

Since childhood, she had been taught to believe in God, and she practiced her faith. She had a relationship with God. Her relationship began early in life. At the age of seven, she attended the store-front Progressive Baptist Church, participating in Sunday School, singing in the youth choir, becoming a junior usher and bonding with other kids from different neighborhoods.

She developed her own personal relationship with her God in a child's manner. As she grew to be a teenager, she strengthened and improved her relationship with God.

As an adult, she considered herself a semi-mature faithful Christian. She was spiritual, a believer, and she had a close relationship with God, but she knew there was room to grow in her faith. Yes, she was a believer, because she knew and experienced the love of God.

She could testify to the goodness of God. She was a faithful Christian who regularly attended church services, paid her offerings, served in ministries, prayed and read the *Bible*, but she craved continual growth in her relationship with God.

In her time of crisis, she would have to renew and lean on the relationship she had with God *and strengthen it!* She knew that the word stated, ***there would be trials and tribulations,*** and yet in a misguided way, she thought she could orchestrate and author which tribulations and trials she would face. Her faith was being stretched, and she had no choice but to strengthen her reliance of trusting and believing.

When she realized her faith was being tested, she assumed she had to be patient and persevere through the challenging time. She would get through it and make it to her destiny. However, she did not expect that arriving at her destination would take as long as it did. Although the *Bible* stated ***there*** *would be trials and tribulations and to wait patiently — John 16:33,* she somehow had thought that she would be exempt of some of the bumps of enduring and waiting, or she could control the ride or at least not have to face so many things at once and certainly not for so long.

She had modeled her life after a script where she played by the rules (the rules she had been taught), stayed out of trouble, went to college, worked hard, married and built a family, joined organizations, served her community, attended church and prayed at night. She assumed doing all those things would reward her with the life that would make her happy and fulfilled. Yet she was at a point where she questioned her previous values and realized she had no control over external factors. She had many questions and knew she was in a valley.

Eventually, she did what any normal human would—she began to ask questions. Did God hear her? Was the abrupt disruption a response of an action? Was it a sign from God? What kind of God was He? What truly was her purpose? What were her gifts? What was she created to do?

The job was gone, her children were grown, and her daily routine was a zigzag. She knew change had arrived and she was living a different type of life. All she wanted was to receive a recognizable sign, to know God was listening to her.

She wanted to know she mattered and an affirmation that God still was looking out for her. She wanted to hear His voice. Never, did she imagine this much disruption or this type of valley. So, she had to reflect, think, believe, and wait. She looked to Him for direction.

Chapter 2

Defeat, Loss and Rejection

You are coming to Christ, who is the living cornerstone of God's temple. He was rejected by people, but he was chosen by God for great honor. — *1 Peter 2:4*

Rejection became a familiar activity for Melissa. The very thing that was her Achilles heel would now be in her face daily: Rejection.

She had to learn to embrace loss and rejection. She had to learn to accept that rejection was not personal but, simply, was a statement that affirmed she was not a good fit for a particular position.

There was something else that God had for her. Rejection served as her guide to maintain a forward focus and keep life moving. *This position is not what God has for me*, she thought. However, the issue was that she was used to being in control of her life, being an achiever, and being successful. It was what she grew accustomed to.

Though she was a believer, she relied on her abilities and did not always practice faith and leave room for God. She had prepared academically— she had sacrificed and worked hard in order to obtain her Bachelor's Degree in Finance and a Master's Degree.

Previously, she always over-prepared in order to avoid being in a position of weakness or vulnerability. However, her situation changed. During challenging circumstances and rejections, she felt very vulnerable. The tables had turned. She would have to rely on her savings and His word. She would have to believe *his grace is sufficient for you, for his power is made perfect in weakness."* — *2 Corinthians 12:9*

Rejection was difficult to accept, because she was feeling more dejected and defeated than she had ever felt or wanted to feel. She often reflected and recounted how, during the last eight years, she had applied and interviewed for over 12 positions. She didn't think much of most of the positions, because she was testing the waters, and she didn't care whether she received the positions or not. But over the last three years—in spite of her education, experience and gifts—when she needed to be able to close a deal and get an offer, she was still not able to achieve her goal.

She was encountering a constant flow of rejection as she reflected on the interview process for the last few positions over the last months.

Position #1

Melissa spoke with a lady in an organization that she belonged to, and it seemed like this interaction was the sign she had been seeking. She thought the interaction perhaps would take her to the new "better door." They talked about subjects, ranging from parenting to current events, and as the discussion continued, Melissa revealed that she was dealing with many things in her life, including the upcoming loss of her job.

Ironically, the lady volunteered, "I am looking for someone to work for my employer, someone with your experience." Melissa thought the woman's reply was perfect, a sign. It was the open door. So excitedly, Melissa proceeded to further describe her background, and the woman seemed more impressed with her skillset, and indicated that Melissa was a perfect match for her employer. They exchanged contact information.

Later, Melissa chatted with her and then interviewed with her and her colleagues. Melissa hoped the woman would be her angel, with a great opportunity on a platter. But nothing came of the conversation or interview. The position did not pan out. Everything went completely quiet, with no additional conversations.

Dr. Lisa A. Reeves

Melissa later thought the "non-offer" was probably for the best. If it had come to fruition, then she would have left her position before they eliminated her job. That would have meant she would not have settled on the separation package, nor the other benefits she eventually did receive. Melissa believed that God was telling her, "This job is not for you. No is the answer."

"My grace is all you need, for my power is greatest when you are weak" — *2 Corinthians 12:9.*

Position #2

This prospect was for an executive position near Melissa's hometown. Her leadership experience would equip her well for this position. She thought it would be a great fit. She had the broad experience to lead a team.

She had worked in all the areas that were needed to run the division. She possessed all the major components of what she thought the job entailed. She even had a strong budgeting background, which was just what this company needed. She was someone who clearly understood the financial picture.

She knew it would be a tough job, because the company was located in a saturated area, a highly competitive area. However, she was eager for the challenge, and she was willing to take the position, even though it had several raised flags.

She felt good when she had the opportunity to interview. It was another nugget—manna for the day, a sign while in the valley.

Things were looking promising. Many things signaled that an offer would soon manifest itself. If an offer did not result from the position, then there was another position that was a possibility. While she interviewed for both these positions, her position in her current job had not ended. She was still going to the office and transitioning out of the workplace.

During the time her current position was phasing out, she received a call to have a telephone interview for position #2.

A few days after the telephone interview, she received a call, asking if she would be interested in coming to interview face-to-face with some of the leadership team. The interview would include 15 people in total. She traveled to the designated off-site campus location for the interview.

She was excited about the opportunity. Upon her arrival, she was caught off-guard, as there was little activity. Actually, the place seemed desolate. Always optimistic, she ignored the sign and maintained her enthusiasm. She was impressed with the thought that she would have a chance to be considered for such an impressive position.

She ignored the red flags, and after a few days passed, she received a call from the head of Human Resources, who indicated Melissa had made it to the finalist round for interviewing. The HR head asked Melissa to come in and interview with the executive senior-level staff and other campus leaders.

It was extremely exciting news! She believed the interview would garner her an offer, since the woman told her there were only two finalists. She prepared intensively for this interview, with research, recommendations and mock interviews.

Though she had received concerning signals along the way, she was ready and excited to take on this role! The day-long interview came, and the process felt good. She presented before the teams, and the president appeared to be impressed. All 50 people throughout the day, including the president, seemed to give her positive feedback and nodded their heads.

The day ended and she wrapped up with the head of HR, where he stated he would be in touch within the following week.

On an interesting note, she had discovered that a good friend's sister was one of the interviewers. The sister shared with her friend that Melissa had done a great job. Melissa thought position #2 was surely going to work out. She had done the interview the last week of November.

In early December, she was poised to travel out of town to visit family. She would get her answer while she was on vacation. She waited excitedly, but when she got the call from HR, she was shocked to hear the news. It was not the response she expected. Position #2 did not come through. It was another rejection.

She did not have an answer for what had just happened. It did not make sense. They seemed to really like her, and she had received excellent feedback. However, they selected someone else. She was surprised by the decision. It was difficult for her to digest the decision, but she had to remember that *God, who is in heaven, does as he wishes. — Psalms 115:3.*

A few months later, she found out who they selected instead. The person who was chosen had worked for a highly visible, well-connected governmental official. The selected candidate was someone who had many corporate contacts. Once she realized who they selected, she quickly understood this individual brought influence from within the state and several corporate entities, and the person could help with partnerships and generate more business, which meant more students.

The institution sought its best interests in an effort to break into a competitive market. She concluded that *she was not supposed to get the position.* The interview was simply an exercise, a hope placeholder to keep her competitive until the next hope opportunity arrived. The process occupied time and gave her practice.

She got over the disappointment and was not hurt or discouraged because she understood this position was not for her. Besides, she had Position #3 in the works. Position #3 did not have half the stress or responsibility she was used to having in a job.

The position was below her capacity, but the position was at a prestigious institution. It would be easy. The job would be a steppingstone, a way to get in the door. Circumstances seemed promising for a job offer.

The person leading the search was someone she had met at a conference. He communicated that he was very impressed with her abilities. At the time of the interview, she interviewed with several individuals and received plenty of positive vibes. Although the position was not at the same level that she had been accustomed to, she thought it would work out while she completed some personal projects.

She met the team and felt good about the interview process. The Thanksgiving holiday was fast-approaching, and a decision would not be made until after the holiday, or in early December. She was traveling and would find out the decision while she was away on vacation.

She expected to receive two positive decisions. However, that was not the situation. For the first position, the director called and indicated that he selected an internal applicant. For the second position, they selected the other finalist.

Neither of the position interviews worked out. When position number three did not work out, she thought, *Wow, another rejection! Two rejections while on vacation. Who gets that?*

The process was becoming concerning and discouraging. Even though she had a hopeful spirit and approached things in a positive manner, she felt she had hit another pothole in the valley. What she despised more than anything was negative-thinking people and rejection, and it appeared rejection was raining down on her.

Was there a target on her back? Did God not want her to work a full-time job? This valley experience was not fun. It was full of disappointment, discouragement and difficulty. Had God forgotten about her?

The experience of rejection, coupled with loss and disappointment, became her journey. Even though she was a believer, she found her faith had weakened, that her faith was being tested. She was human, after all. She questioned where God was amid this experience.

She did not have a road map for getting out of the valley, which was filled with ditches and potholes. She would have to learn how to live amongst the pitfalls, relying on God, and navigating during the dark, discouraging and uncertain times.

She would find solace in the scripture that encouraged, *be glad about this, even though it may now be necessary for you to be sad for a while because of the many kinds of trials you suffer. Their purpose is to prove that your faith is genuine. Even gold, which can be destroyed is tested by fire; and so, your faith, which is much more precious than gold must also be tested, so that it may endure. Then you will receive praise and glory and honor on the Day when Jesus Christ is revealed — 1 Peter 6-7.* This scripture gave her comfort as she approached each new day with wonder and concern.

At that point in time, December 2017, she was approaching the end of her job assignment. She had a generous severance package and decided to pull back from aggressively searching for a job and instead focus on completing her PhD and listening to God.

She felt she had more control in that area. She could research and write and believe she had power over something in her life. She also realized that the time when she was not working made it easier for her to conduct her research. The research for her PhD was focused on spirituality and self-determination of black women.

For her research, she would have to dedicate time to travel, conduct interviews, gather data, analyze data, produce findings and write. Her research gave her hope and strengthened her faith, giving her opportunities to hear how the power of God helped others. She knew God showed no favoritism. *God is no respecter of person — Acts 10:34.* What He does for one, He can do for others.

She would have to learn to depend on scripture and hear God in her vulnerable state, during rejection and disappointment. She relied on Matthew 21:42, *knowing the stone that the builders rejected has become the cornerstone; this was the Lord's doing and it is marvelous in her eyes.*

She came to know that the scripture spoke truth. It fortified her faith. She accepted her place in the valley, and this would be a "boot camp" experience. She would have to train her mind, body and spiritual being in order to get to the mountaintop.

She decided that *she would boast all the more gladly of her weaknesses, so that the power of Christ may rest upon her — 2 Corinthians 12:9.* She took the rejection as an indication that God was leading her in a different direction. She had to wait patiently.

Chapter 3

Change Comes

Everything on earth has its own time and its own season —
Ecclesiastes 3:1
No one knows, however, when that day or hour will come
neither the angels in heaven, nor the Son; only the Father
knows — Mark 13:32

Melissa was experiencing a major change in her life. She quickly realized that when it is time for change, then it is time to act. The change will not be sudden. There will be signs that lead to change. She knew the scripture said, *Be on watch, be alert, for you do not know when the time will come — Mark 13:33.* In reality, a person must be willing to change in order to grow.

Nothing remains the same. People's lives are constantly changing, intentionally or unintentionally, and yet they are receiving signs along the journey to prepare them for the next phase. Each moment is preparation for the next moment.

These moments may be encounters with people who speak a message or state a phrase that seems to have meaning or provoke a sudden thought in one's mind. Even a rainbow in the sky will give someone a message.

Each thing matters, and collectively they are signs. Either a person pays attention to the sign or that individual will, intentionally, be caught off-guard. Regardless of one's state of mind, when it is time for change, there will be signs. There are sometimes *wonders,* and yes, when it is time, there will be a change.

But it will not be totally unexpected. *God will testify with you, both by signs and wonders and by various miracles and*

by gifts of the Holy Spirit according to His own will —
Hebrews 2:4.

When there are signs, we have the opportunity to take notice and do something, or we will wait until we have no choice and are forced to do something. The good news is that we have the ability to choose, for God has given us free will. *He has now given us a choice between a blessing and a curse. When all these things have happened to you, and you are living among the nations where the Lord your God has scattered you, you will remember the choice He has given you — Deuteronomy 30:1.*

Initially, the signs will first appear as quiet thoughts, like goldfish that are calmly swimming by in a bowl, thoughts that highlight perhaps one should consider doing something different. Then the signs will become stronger. There will be things that one notices more plainly that initially seem to be coincidental or happenstance.

When this happened to her, she shrugged and thought, *hmmm, that was interesting!* but she still chose not to take it seriously. Later, the signs occurred more frequently and intensely. They were affirmations. At that point, she hesitated, stunned and unsure if she could or wanted to leave her comfortable space.

And she was afraid. She was stuck. Finally, she waited until the signs became so disruptive that she was left with no choice but to act, because the need for change had been thrust upon her and she knew she had to make adjustments.

The signs came as touches to prepare her for growth or for what was to come. She had to remember that the signs were challenges and opportunities to step out on faith. They were masked as storms of life, valleys of difficulty, things that would force a person to face fears or demons.

People grow by dealing with the uncomfortable situations. She had to become innovative or stay stagnate, or wither away. That would be her choice. God tells us, *Let the wise listen and add to their learning and let the discerning get guidance — Proverbs 1:5.* Your signs and wonders will come, and it is no surprise to your heavenly Father. They are to draw you closer to him.

The change is an opportunity to connect or to strengthen one's relationship with his/her heavenly father. The sign is an opportunity to see hope in the midst of darkness. It is a time to recreate and to remember there is something bigger for a person's future and that God has created each individual for a reason. The change is an opportunity to explore that he/she would ordinarily not have given a second thought.

The change represents a time to believe, to remember and to **trust in God's plan for your life — Proverbs 3:5-6.** God has a plan for us. He tells us what our lives will be and how we should not rely on our own understanding. The scripture tells us about our future. It tells us about hope and gives us inspiration.

God tells us that He is the master planner. *For He knows the plans He has for us, they are plans for good and not for disaster, plans to give us a future and a hope — Jeremiah 29:11.* Our job is to remember, believe, trust, create and live.

But what happens when someone cannot pull it together? It seems that day—and our entire future, does not come with good. The manifestation of the dream has not taken place. That's when doubt creeps in and one questions when his/her time will come?

Repeatedly she saw disappointment. Yes, she may have seen some flurries of prosperity, like snow flurries of favor, but not the accumulation that she hoped for or what she believed she was promised. She pondered, *how does someone continue to maintain joy and peace? How does one continue to survive when it seems that she has been denied, repeatedly?*

Remember God says, **at the time I have decided, my words will come true. You can trust what I say about the future. It may take a long time but keep on waiting and it will happen. — Habakkuk 2:3.**

Chapter 4

The Beginning

For we are his workmanship, created in Christ Jesus for good works, which God prepared beforehand, that we should walk in them. — Ephesians 2:10

Profile

She identified herself in many ways, including the following descriptions: a Christian, African American, wife, mother, sister, educated individual, administrator, and middle-class member.

She was born in the inner-city of a Midwest town, from a lower social economic-class family. From humble beginnings, she described her experience growing up as being "upper-poor," which was a term she created to describe her family's social economic status and existence.

She was from a family of five children, plus a niece who lived within the household. Through black self-determination, her paternal grandparents, despite the unknown, left the racial prejudice of the South with the hopes of finding a better life in the North—a faith walk.

They were part of the big migration in the late 1940s, moving from the scorching summers of Georgia to the incredibly frigid winters of Ohio. The shared culture of blacks involving poverty, sharecropping, lynching and unjust treatment made it easy for her grandparents to have the self-determination to leave the racially-prejudiced South. Their hope fueled dreams and planted the seeds for the harvest to come.

After arriving up North, her dad attended Central High School. Prior to graduating, he returned to Georgia to retrieve his teenage love. She left high school, and together they travelled up north with love, a dream, and hope of creating a life together, a better life than what the discriminating South had offered.

They built their dreams up north. Her parents had not completed high school. Thus the employment they were offered centered around low-paying factory jobs. So they persevered, with hard work and dignity, in a different world, a world far removed from the more familiar Jim Crow South. They were in a new place where they would raise their children with the love, in an urban neighborhood that contained families and friends who looked out for one another.

She was the youngest of five children; her oldest sibling was 17 years older than she was, and the sibling next to the oldest child—her brother, was ten years older than she was. Given the age disparity, she often felt she had different experiences growing up than they did.

Sometimes, it appeared to her that instead of two parents, she had several, along with a lesser number of siblings. Her oldest sister had a daughter who was close to her age. Her niece was one year younger, so they were raised as sisters and did many things together.

She and her niece shared the same bed and had many of the same friends. Some people assumed that her niece was her younger sister, until her older sister and daughter moved to their own home and the girls were no longer together as much.

The family grew up in a modest 1,400 square-foot single three-bedroom, one-bathroom family bungalow, built in 1916. It had a single car detached garage. The home was in an all-black lower-class neighborhood.

Although her parents did not have high school diplomas or professional advisors to shape their thinking, they were savvy enough to figure out a way to obtain a home through a land contract. The banks typically refused to lend to black folks who lived in what were classified as "redlined neighborhood districts," where many other black families lived.

People who lived in these areas were considered to "high-risk" because of slow payment or non-payment of their debts, so mortgages were not an option. Since her parents were unable to acquire a mortgage to purchase homes, land contracts became their vehicle to homeownership.

It was a sacrifice they took on proudly to acquire a single-family dwelling for their children. This sacrifice of acquiring a land contract meant they owned their home, which was purchased at a higher-than-market-value price. The land contract rate of paying for a house and not having the tax benefits meant that Mr. Williams, the landlord, would have that luxury of building wealth for his family for too long.

Being upper-poor, her family lived in poverty, but because both of her parents lived in the household and generated some income, they were not poor enough for full government subsidies. She often thought being "upper-poor" was worse than being "poor-poor," since if the family did not budget for expenses precisely, or if there a mishap, a utility shutoff would likely occur.

For most of her life, the bill paying went as planned, and sometimes there were extras for the holidays. Melissa never had a Christmas without presents, Christmas lights, a real Christmas tree or an Easter without a new church outfit and an Easter basket.

As she reflected, she realized her childhood was pretty good. They never skipped a meal, never had to go to a shelter for housing and never had to go to a food bank. It was a simple, basic life, with her mother and father doing their best to live a life of laughter, peace and joy.

Occasionally, they managed a family cookout, a ride to Edgewater park, working in the yard, or just sitting on the front porch, talking with the neighbors. They lived a life where her parents kept the yard manicured, shoveled the snow, and attempted to make ends meet while they raised the family. It was a life where they extracted a fraction of the American dream and a piece of dignity.

It was a non-extravagant life, one where she did not wear fashionable clothes. Her parents drove an old used car that usually needed some sort of work to be done. She remembered the one car where the engine burned excessive oil and the muffler was so loud that neighbors could hear the car two blocks before they arrived.

It was humiliating and embarrassing as a young child, trying to figure a way out of these noticeable badges of poverty, including being driven in a rundown car.

Growing up, she had not travelled to adventurous places or any other places, nor had she flown on an airplane. Her parents were not able to afford those types of luxuries. It would not be until she was married and had her own children that she enjoyed such experiences.

In her childhood home, her parents provided love, a place to play jacks on the bathroom floor and kickball in the backyard. She had security, food, a garden and the basics to acquire the self-awareness that enabled her to believe that one day, she could make a difference—in her circumstances, in the world and in the fulfillment of her own dream.

Her father worked hard in the hot steel mill, and her mother worked earnestly in a sewing factory. They arose early in the mornings. Each workday, her mom took the number 15 bus from E. 116th and Union to Broadway near E. 55th street, and her dad reluctantly drove the loud used car to Republic Steel.

She remembered her parents' conversations about their non-airconditioned, close-quarters places of employment. The steel mill was a hard and dangerous environment for laborers. She remembered her dad's stories about the unbearable conditions in proximity to the hot molten steel pouring from the furnace.

Often, he came home with swollen burn marks on his body, resulting from the mills' hot temperatures and the workers' contact with flying bits of burning hot steel. It was no wonder he did not look forward to working the night shift or any shift. His job was beyond hard labor.

Her mom left for work to go to the sewing factory on Broadway before Melissa woke up and got out of bed. On rare occasions, her mother was able to get a car ride with other factory workers rather than riding the bus. Once she arrived at work, her job was to sew buttons and buttonholes on clothing. She worked an honest day's work to help support her family. Factory and domestic labor jobs provided income for those who did not have a skill or education. Such memories remained sketched in her mind, reminding her to work hard and to be diligent in her studies.

Being the youngest of five children, she often observed her older siblings' behavior and thought, *I sure don't want to make the same types of mistakes I saw them make.* Over time, she decided to use their actions as lessons so that and everything in her world would be okay, or at least different than theirs.

Her mother allowed her to get involved in different types of activities, so this youngest child in the family participated in after-school programs, community youth programs, took dance lessons, and she attended the store front church, to which she was driven weekly by her school-teacher and her family.

Her inner-city experiences and choices were different than those of her siblings. She gained exposure to different activities and people. She saw that some people lived in different kinds of housing and owned possessions—unlike those her family had, thought differently, and attended different types of schools. She realized that inequities and injustices existed amongst black people.

She had fond memories of visiting her maternal grandparents down south in August of every year. Her daddy rented a car for the ride. The family packed into a rented station wagon with a marked AAA map and headed to the rich red soil of Georgia to visit Big Ma, Big Daddy, Ant Lu, Uncle Oscar, and loads of cousins. It was such a fun time.

Her cousins took her and her niece to amusement parks, the corner store to get ice cream, and to hang out. The ritual of seeing her mom going back home was something she anticipated. Mom was frying chicken, buying loaves of bread, fixing bologna sandwiches, cutting up cantaloupe, watermelon and honey dew for her fruit salad.

They packed the cooler the night before, and half-asleep, they left at 3:00 in the morning for a 12-hour drive. The chicken was perfectly fried, wrapped in wax paper and aluminum foil and packed in the basket, always the right temperature to eat with a slice of *Wonder* bread, an apple, and some *Better Made* potato chips. There would be a picnic midday at a rest area along I-75 at a clean rest stop. If the family timed it right, they would be somewhere near Chattanooga, Tennessee, by lunch time.

She understood that 3:00 a.m., was the desired time to leave for the trip, since her dad would have gotten just enough sleep to drive throughout the rest of the night while the kids slept in the car. Leaving at that ungodly hour would provide a bit of peace for her mom and dad during a 12-hour ride with children, who quickly became restless and got bored during the ride.

Later, she understood very early morning was the best time to travel, due to the family not being able to stay or afford to be in hotels or go to restaurants as they entered the South. It was also a time when not many state patrol men were out and would not unnecessarily stop and harass them.

At an early age, she was identified as being a bright child. She skipped kindergarten and went straight to first grade. In the fall of third grade, she was transferred to a different school district for a more advanced school curriculum.

On Monday thru Friday, the seven-year-old would walk alone, four blocks to take the number 50 bus to get to school. She felt adventurous and thought she had been given a gift of hope for a better life. The daily journey did not frighten her. What she did not know was that her mom had reached out to the business owners along her path. Her mother had reached out to Kirby at the Corner Store, Mr. White at the Barber Shop and Henry at the Cleaners. Each morning at around eight, they would watch out for her and greet her with a smile and wave as she walked past their storefront windows. They were her guide to the bus stop.

As her mother learned of her academic potential, she encouraged her baby girl to strengthen her knowledge. Throughout her schooling, Mom would enroll her in various after school programs.

While in the second grade, she met a young teacher who invited her to their family store front church. She felt special, and she loved that each Sunday, this family picked her up and allowed her to participate in Sunday School and Church Service.

It was then that her Christian values began forming. Not only were the seeds of Jesus being planted, but she was also exposed to other families, whose lifestyles, values and experiences were different from her family's.

From the age of 6 to 17, she attended the church and made friends with others who were black like she was and who had different lifestyles. It was then that she began to see "different classes."

Later, she discovered from her friends at church and other programs that their schools were "different and better" than hers, even though she attended a more advanced school than the one in her neighborhood. Those who were in her same grade did work that was more advanced than hers in the urban school district.

This realization encouraged her to learn all she could from her school and do her best. She was ecstatic when the hard work paid off and she had the opportunity to attend college. Though her family, being upper poor, could not afford to pay for college, and she did not qualify for a lot of financial assistance, she had an aunt who agreed to provide some money for her to go away to college.

She did well in her high school, though in college she struggled. She realized that the education she received in her urban public school did not prepare her as well as others had been prepared, that segregated schools did not provide the same type of rigor and curriculum.

During college, she had to work hard and be diligent about getting help. These work-ethic habits she had picked up from her parents were useful while undertaking her bachelor's degree. When she graduated from college, her parents were beaming with pride, since she was the first in their family to earn a degree. Soon thereafter, she moved out of state to work in her chosen field.

For many years, she thought she was living a good life with her husband. She considered herself blessed and was thankful. In her daily life, she was cheerful, put together and at peace. Many commented that she was doing just fine, if not better than that.

She was married to a loving man and was a mother of two smart adult children who were out of the house, and she was in good health. For years, she had worked at a job that significantly provided financially for her family and was somewhat fulfilling. Her work was satisfying, and she had received several promotions. Her job, along with her husband's, provided resources that enabled her family to live comfortably.

They were following the path they had plotted. She raised her family, participated in organizations and had a church home. She had a faith that was steadfast and comfortable. She believed in God, and God had shown His love and favor toward her. Blessed with friends who supported her, friends she travelled with, and acquaintances she trusted, she was grateful for the life she lived.

Her life was, in no way, the oppressive lifestyle that her parents had endured in the South. There were no significant events that she saw as being horrible or earth-shattering. She lived life with love, and she was grateful for being mentally sound and physically fit.

Yet over the last five to seven years, things had changed. She felt unsettled and recognized signs that something was not quite right. She eventually came to understand that she was entering a valley moment.

Chapter 5

Living Amongst the Signs

This shall be the sign to you from the LORD, that the LORD will do this thing that He has spoken. — *Isaiah 38:7*

While in the valley, there were many incidents that occurred. Were they messages, coincidences or bad luck? In a short span of time—the loss of a parent, the loss of a job, a car accident, the loss of a parent-in-law, the loss of a sibling, a sudden illness amongst her other siblings, and illness amongst close friends?

When she began her valley moment, she did not know if it was a test of her faith or a curse. Was this her "Job" moment, with the heavens watching? *Was it her time of suffering, weeping and mourning, as stated in John 16:20?* The valley seemed to surround her in every possible way.

It was a difficult period. Her heart ached and there were weeks of nights of restless sleep where she felt alone. Often, she awoke in the middle of the night, enduring long hours of endless sleep, sometimes sweating and pondering her current situation.

She was certain all the grief and stress brought the onset of menopause, which she believed, since was no explanation for its sudden arrival other than her over-ripe age. When it rained, it poured! She wondered were all the occurrences simply happenstances or was it her time to be in the valley?

While in her valley, she prayed and asked that her faith be made stronger, *please help me to have even more faith — Mark 9:24.* Getting accustomed to breathing and living in the valley was harder than she ever expected. People that she was used to being with and calling were no longer available.

She had more hot flashes than ever before, constantly experiencing hot and night sweats. There was uncertainty and loneliness. She realized that, while in the valley, it was not unusual to have doubt and unbelief. She was human and was experiencing natural physical emotions.

More than ever, she needed a miraculous blessing from God, as she was in a place that was uncomfortable and where she lacked control. She prayed and asked that God not leave her in this valley, but she asked Him to carry her to her mountain top. She thought of the scripture from *Jeremiah 29:11 — For I know the plans I have for you declares the Lord, plans to prosper you and not to harm you plans to give you hope and a future.*

She needed hope and a future to survive in the valley. She needed to cling firmly to faith and hope. She knew that, if she did not stay grounded in her faith, she could lose out via stress and worry.

Fortunately, between the tears and sadness, her sense of humor made an appearance and peeked through. She sarcastically chuckled and said, "Now I understand what it means to wake up in your right mind." First—it meant you got sleep, and therefore, woke up; second—at least your mind was *halfway* functioning!

Later, she realized the statement was Biblical and that to be *in your right mind was a benefit. — 2 Corinthians 5:13.* She also realized that having a personal fan was helpful for the flashes.

Through these life challenges and changes, she came to appreciate that finding her peace and joy was priceless and Biblical. During her praying moments, she practiced *giving all her worries and cares to God, for he cared about her. — 1 Peter 5:7*

Even more so now, she leaned on the promises of the Bible and was intentional about what she was thinking, what words she was speaking, and who was in her ear. She paid attention to what she did to occupy her time. It all mattered, and she had to be intentional.

She knew that the persons she surrounded herself by and spoke with could mean life or death. She knew that *letting the Spirit control her mind would lead to life and peace.* — *Romans 8: 6*

She realized that when she again looked for employment, she needed to exercise more, participate in self-help classes and volunteer. Her routine had changed so that she was sitting more and eating differently. These intentional thoughts and actions helped her while she was in the valley.

She understood that she needed to have peace to help her to get to the next nugget of glory to overcome uncertainty. She understood that it was purely *a gift to have peace of mind and heart. It was a gift from God that the world could not give. She had to resist from being troubled and being afraid.* — *John 14:27.*

She wasn't going to let the natural things and sinful nature capture her mind and thoughts. She wasn't going to allow the shadows of life to overpower her, since she knew that course would lead to death. God's word stated *don't worry about anything; instead, pray about everything. Tell God what you needed and thank him for all he had done.* — *Philippians 4:6.*

That is the course that she pursued. She spoke loudly and often to God... about everything. Despite her adversity, she cultivated a thankful spirit. She learned to meditate on His words and find peace. It was hard but, slowly, she came to recognize and accept that *there would be all kinds of trials and tribulations, but she would find her peace in God.* — *John 16:33*

These life challenges and changes were signs of the shift for what was to come. It was all in preparation. The signs mattered.

A Prayer...

She often prayed, and she made her prayers clear, though they were often done quickly. Though she knew God stated, **wait patiently on the Lord — Psalm 37:7**, she was waiting with expectancy and was ready for a response. Regardless of the instructions, she was just a bit impatient.

With so many things going on in her life, she just wanted some stability and a clear sign. So when irregular things continued manifest, she asked God to help her to accept all the occurrences and interpret the messages. She wanted to be in God's will and did not want to miss hearing or seeing a sign.

Often, she would pray, *"please God— make it clearer for me. I want to know it is you who is talking!"*. Being in the valley was not easy, and she was becoming a bit skeptical. You see, though she was a practicing Christian, she questioned many things… she had a tendency to over-analyze activities.

She was still working on complete trust with God. Although she was a believer, she was a believer who was still developing and growing, a worshipper, but sometimes a worshipper who worried.

Lord— *"please **help me with my unbelief, doubt, and fear**. Send me clearer messages,"* she often stated. She was used to being in control—or at least *thinking she was in control* and planning her life.

While she had always controlled her surroundings to protect herself from humiliation, rejection, embarrassment, and hurt, she did not realize that the rejection often was protection, and God was leading her in a different direction.

She wanted to be sure of things, but in the valley, she was unsure of most things. She knew that, as a true believer, she would have to learn to be comfortable with the unknown and surrender more to God, believe His word, and act upon it. But in her mind, she justified her mustard seed faith that was still developing, still evolving—a *believer-in-progress*.

The signs were coming often, and sometimes they came directly or indirectly. She received a sign that nudged her to present her research in different formats. Her research topic covered a stronger content of spirituality. She wanted to get her research out to a wider audience, beyond academics and scholars, but she was unsure how to accomplish it.

On one occasion, a sign appeared on television. While watching, she realized the show was based on a research study. She had been thinking that the content of her research was worthy of a documentary, or a series of some sort or a book. She wanted to write a book, but she knew nothing about that sort of writing.

Then, during the broadcast, there was a commercial pertaining to a Christian Faith Publisher. The advertisement was a call to persons who had "never written a book and wanted to know how to get started." She wondered if the documentary and ad appeared as a coincidence, a happenstance, or a sign given to her from God. She had been thinking about writing a book for over a year and needed help sharing her spiritual message with a larger audience.

It seemed like small separate incidences—happenstance, but in actuality, God had been revealing himself to her while she was in the valley. She had often asked, "God *please tell me what you would have me to do?*" *"What is my gift? What did you create me to be? Do you hear my prayers? Please make it clear to me."*

She wanted to hear from God. She wanted to be *in* His will. She believed that her gift was to motivate others and to give hope through the promises of God. She had a passion for education, but she was not sure about how to combine her passion and skill set. She understood that there were different ways to share His message beyond using traditional methods at the church podium. Little by little, she was able to see how God was guiding her footsteps.

As she reflected, she believed God had been speaking and giving her the answers for many years all along. She just needed to slow down, to hear and accept the messages. Throughout her life, God had communicated with her in many ways, with signs and wonders. She needed to recognize the signs that were splattered in the midst of her daily activity. She needed to slow her pace, or in her case, shut it down to hear what was in her gut. She was so busy and consumed with daily life that she often ignored thoughts and signs, or she was just too consumed to pursue them.

So it was not surprising that, though the valley was quiet, it brought her a sense of peace. She began to hear… when she did not get caught up in her feelings. She could think in the valley. She could dream. She knew she had been anxious in her constructed life and wanted to do something different, though she just was unsure of what and how.

In the valley, she *saw* God and felt Him coddling her. In the valley, it was easier to connect with God and dream. The challenge was she would have to rely on faith, to take a chance, to do something different—to be bold, creative and unafraid of failure. It became clearer to her that, in order for her to get out of the valley, she had to boldly align herself with God's will and accept the signs and stop relying on what was familiar.

Unfortunately, the path for Melissa to get out of the valley had to be through rejection, delays and setbacks. She often fell back into old familiar habits. She reverted to what was familiar, which resulted in rejection. She circled the same block many times, going after what she thought was a sure match or sure thing, and again, she would be rejected.

It did not matter how many times or ways she asked or presented the request. If it was not meant for her, "no" was the answer—the door did not open. Thus she came to believe that, for her to grow in her faith, hear God, and become closer to Him, she had to learn the lessons of rejection.

Rejection was the journey from the valley to the mountain top. Rejection was necessary to her experience. She realized that sometimes rejection was even meant to protect her. At other times, the answer "no" was just because God had a different plan for her, another direction.

And often the answer "no" was because she didn't get what "no" meant the first time. And if she repeatedly returned with the same issue or question, dressed in a different outfit and expecting a different answer, it did not matter. It was not His desire for her. "No."

I Got Your Attention

God had a way of getting her attention without forewarning. On a Wednesday in January at around 5:30 p.m., God abruptly disrupted her evening drive. Melissa and a dear friend were driving into the city to attend a meeting downtown with an organization to mentor women in poverty.

It was a pleasant day, considering it was the winter season in January—not much snow and the roads were clear. The temperature hovered around 30 degrees. Prior to the ride, She had debated if she would drive, and she had thought, *why not?* She was already in her car and there was no snow or ice. It was easy to continue driving, so she decided to swing by and pick up Lila.

When they pulled up to the traffic light and stopped, waiting for the light to change, they suddenly heard the sound of metal colliding with metal. They had been hit! A woman's car had T-boned her car—on the driver's car door, which startled both her and Lila.

The driver came out of a hospital parking lot. She had seen the other driver from the corner of her eye as she looked forward and talked with Lila. They both saw the car approaching and assumed she saw them. Replaying the situation in her mind, she thought, *I saw her. The lady had to see me!* In the last instant, she swerved and blew the horn. Too late! BAM! Her car had been hit!

WHAM! She was in a daze. She felt the impact. Her driver's car door was definitely hit. It was dented in so that she could feel wind blowing in through the damaged metal. There was no debating it. They had been solidly hit

She exited the car, dazed from the impact, and she continued to wonder how the driver didn't see her. Part of her wanted to puff up, tell the driver off and act foolish. *What the heck was this woman thinking?* Being from the inner city, she chuckled as she thought she could still act thug-like, which was a far stretch from her spiritual praying and kind personality.

However, she still "straightened up" and walked like she was straight from the hood of Cleveland, until she noticed the petite stature of an elderly black woman, getting out of her car and walking towards her. The woman's demeanor instantly calmed her, seeing an older woman, who could have been her mother, or an angel.

She was confused. She didn't know how to respond. The lady asked, "Are you okay?" and said, "I didn't see you. I will *pay* you. I don't want this to go through my insurance. I will pay you. Trust me."

Was the woman asking her not to go through her insurance? *Was the woman crazy?* she thought. *I don't know her. Is this older lady trying to hustle me? Who is she and what is she talking about?* As they both looked at her car, there was no denying the damage.

When they walked over to the older woman's car, and there were one or two scratches. It didn't appear that her car had even been in an accident. Both commented on how little damage had been done to the second car. Was the accident an example of God getting her attention, or was it a test?

From the looks of her car, it had been in an unfortunate accident that happened at the hands of an older lady. Certainly there would be expenses and the car obviously needed body work. Both got into the older woman's car. With her phone in hand, she asked the woman for her driver's license.

After the nervous woman fumbled through her pocketbook to find her materials, she gathered her driver's license and insurance card. When she looked at the woman's driver's license to take a picture, she noticed in amazement that the woman's last name was Bridges—which was her own maiden name. Then she noticed that the woman's birth month was the month of her daughter's birthday and her birthday was the day of her son's birthday. These random facts seemed more than oddly coincidental. Did it mean anything? Who was this lady?

Her attention was sparked! This lady could have been a relative of hers! Then the woman looked her in the eyes and said, "Won't You Trust Me?"

The manner of that gesture seemed spiritual to Melissa— far greater than her saying the words. She literally understood the words and their meaning and the promise of not letting this incident go through her insurance company.

The lady even mentioned that she had just gotten a new insurance policy with a different company, but what she heard was something far greater than those words.

Yes, her words meant she didn't want her insurance rates to go up. She likely had a rate that was already astronomical because she lived in the city and was elderly. But it was as if she was someone else who was being used as a conduit. *Won't You Trust Me?* She heard the question, but she interpreted as something spiritual. *Won't You Trust God?*

Still reeling, she called her husband. Not surprising, he quickly and firmly stated, "Call the police and file a police report." He was not feeling spiritual or calming or trusting. In his alpha protective way, he had given her a stern directive.

So she got out the car, returned to hers and called the police. She understood the protocol she was supposed to follow: call the police and respect her husband. But something did not feel right. When Lila asked her if she was alright, she affirmed that she needed to call the police.

Reassuringly, Lila explained that a report could be filed at a later time, that it did not have to be done in the moment. She pondered for a second but then dialed the number for the police. Response to the ringing took what seemed to be forever. The operator commenced to ask her several questions. *Where are you? What side of the road are you on? What city are you in? Is anyone hurt?* There were too many questions for Melissa, so she became irritated.

She imagined a 911 operator would already have some of these answers. *Don't they have a GPS tracking system?* The operator said that she was on the boarder of two cities and she had to transfer her to the proper city police to process her call.

There was nothing about the call that felt right or was easy. Instead, it felt odd and clumsy. Once she was transferred, the police said they would send a car right over, but she and the other driver needed to move from out the middle of street to a safer space. She asked the lady to pull over to the nearby shopping plaza and wait.

She sat in her car, still digesting what happened and waited for the police. She called another friend who owned an insurance agency to explain the situation and asked her about filing a police report a later time. She asked, "How does the report impact someone's insurance rate?"

Her friend replied that the claim would be "a double-hit." She didn't know what that meant. The friend continued that, "once the police report is filed, the woman will be ticketed, get points, and she will have to pay. Once the woman renews her insurance, they will pull her record and see that she has points from an accident and her rates will go up, a double-hit!"

The friend then asked, "Do you trust her?" Melissa was becoming weary of the "trust" question. "Yes, I trust her." Her friend then suggested that Melissa should not file the report immediately, but she should get all the woman's information. "If she doesn't pay, *then* go file the police report," which is what Melissa did. Lila called the police back and cancelled the request. She returned to the lady's car and indicated that she would "work with her."

Melissa decided she would trust, Mrs. Bridges. Melissa had been praying a lot and had asked God to guide her and show her things. She was at a different place in her life. She was seeing and hearing God differently, more clearly. She knew God had been protecting and working with her. And when she heard the woman say, "Won't You Trust Me?" it felt like a message from God saying, "I know this is crazy, but relax and enjoy the ride. This is some of my finer work." So, sitting in her car, she told the woman her decision and said she would trust her. The lady thanked her and assured her that she would pay her once she got an estimate. She thought to herself, *I would never recommend anyone do this.* But she decided to trust her, and the next day, she took her car to get an estimate.

Putting It All Together

Earlier in the week, she had begun thinking seriously started thinking about writing a book. She was still intentionally and diligently following up on work leads, but she was grappling with believing in a bigger dream. She wanted to write a book on the topic from her research (faith and spirituality and self-determination) and have a docu-series or even a movie to present the stories.

She had even written her dream down on her prayer wall. During that week, she had decided to have faith, to take the leap and just do it.

There had been enough nudges to move her forward. On the Monday before the accident, she had, in her quiet moments, in her inner thoughts, been listening to and talking with God. She felt directed to look up, research and write a few things on paper regarding television networks that possibly would be interested in this type of idea. She googled networks and wrote down four possibilities: Lifetime, Own, Hallmark and Netflix.

On the Tuesday preceding the accident, while sitting in her office area, being still, the holy spirit directed her to chat with a tv producer, executive or writer. She needed to speak with someone who had authority in this area, someone who knew the business, who made decisions--someone who understood. So she jotted down *"Chat with TV executive producer or writer."* On Wednesday, she got in the accident and the lady simply stated, "Won't you trust me?"

After the accident and collecting the lady's information, she proceeded to go on to the meeting, driving down the expressway with wind blowing and whistling in her car and still in a bit of a daze.

What had just happened? After the meeting and dropping off her friend, she went home. The first thing her husband asked was, "Did you file a police report?" She walked upstairs in exhaustion and did not reply.

Her husband went outside and examined the car. Then he returned and asked, "Are you okay?" After a nod, he summarized, "That was a hard hit. Your door will need to be replaced. It is going to cost about $3000. I hope you filed a police report."

She quietly admitted that she had not filed the report and that she would handle it the next day. He sarcastically reminded her about the accident their son had over the summer—about how a police report was not filed, and as a result, the person who hit the car did not pay for the damages.

All she could think about was that the lady—who had the last name of Bridges and whose birth month and day was related to those of her children. She had said, "Won't You Trust Me?" It was a long day, so with limited energy remaining, all she could do was go to bed.

The next day, she got out of bed early to quickly go to the car dealership. Her husband insisted she should call him once she got the quote and to not meet anyone in the city to get money. He was concerned about her safety and still suspect about the whole situation, but he knew she would do what she thought made sense.

After pulling into to the dealership garage, she met a pleasant service technician who asked what she needed. She said she needed an estimate on her car that had been damaged an accident. She explained that she would not be dealing with an insurance company, that she would instead, would be dealing with the person who hit her car.

After exchanging pleasantries, she turned over her keys and wandered around the dealership. While filling the time browsing, she encountered a salesman who inquired about her lease status.

When he had completed the estimate, the service person found her and shared that the damage repairs would cost about $3000. The estimate was in line with what her husband had suggested. She thought, *hmmm, he was right.*

When the technician asked how she would be working with her insurance company, she asked why he would need to know that? He responded that the person who hit her would "not" be paying her. She thought it was an odd observation, wondering if he knew something that she didn't.

She repeated that the humble elderly woman said she would cover the costs, but the technician sarcastically responded, "they all say they will pay— until they find out how much, and then they don't. People have good intentions, but they do not pay. Typically, they can't."

Melissa thought that he would have at least given her an ounce of hope. Though seeing her distraught look, and out of a sense of pity, he half-heartedly amended, "Well, every blue moon there may be a payment, but don't get your hopes up." Then he asked, "Did you file a police report?" In disgust, she thought, *Oh, not that again!*

Shaking his head, the service technician looked at her and said, "You'll probably be working with your insurance company. This is a no-fault state, you know. Your insurance company will be covering this, because she will not pay you."

Another service tech agreed and echoed the same sentiment. "You'll need to file a claim with your insurance company. He's right; Michigan's a no-fault state." He felt the need to repeat the statement.

While I had mentioned earlier in our conversation that I was not from Michigan, the technician retorted in a sarcastic tone, "Rather than believe me, call her and tell her the amount of the repairs."

She felt it was a dare. So she did. She called the lady but did not get an answer. Still not moved by the comments from the repair tech, she left a message. While sitting in their presence, the elderly woman returned her call.

She had been in her basement and did not hear the telephone ringing. She said anxiously, "I've been hanging around the house waiting for your call and wanted to know the price of the repairs. What is the cost?" Once Melissa told her the amount was $3,000, the woman seemed surprised. "I didn't expect it to be that much!"

She explained what the repairs required and all the separate items that needed to be done to the car in order for it to be back in its previous condition. The woman asked to hear the amount again and asked, "please repeat it. slowly." The senior citizen wanted to make certain she had written the precise amount exactly because she needed to go to her credit union to withdraw the money.

Inwardly and outwardly, she smiled, because both the men thought she was being naïve and that receiving that $3,000 was something that would never happen in her lifetime. During the call, the woman asked her to please meet her on Greenfield, north of 9-mile, which was just slightly beyond the northern border of the city.

Recalling what her husband had warned about not meeting anyone in the city to get money, she reasoned that, technically, the proposed destination was *not* in the city. "It's one mile *north* of the city, so I'll go to meet her there."

In fact, they met within a couple of hours of the call. She reasoned she would rather her husband come home from work to see that she had taken care of business as she said she would, with a check in hand.

Besides, Melissa was still trusting the lady who had the last name of her maiden name and whose birth month and day was the same as her kids. Melissa remembered she said, "Won't You Trust Me?". Besides, she had selected their meeting spot at a restaurant, and that certainly seemed harmless.

They were scheduled to meet at 12:30 p.m. at Panera Bread. She thought, *What crimes happen around high-noon at Panera Bread?* Since there were none she could think of, she went to the location that had been designated. Unfortunately, when she arrived, there was no Panera Bread. She drove by the location twice.

As she slowly drove by the second time, her phone rang and a voice on the other end said, "I am so sorry, but the restaurant is not there anymore. I just saw you pass by. Please turn around and come back." Crazy as it sounds, she did return and once she returned, she saw Ms. Bridges, standing waiting where the Panera Bread used to be located. Ms. Bridges jumped into her car.

It was in Southfield at an Event by Accident

They talked for two and a half hours. The lady fascinated her. She was almost 80, and She was intrigued by the woman's energy, enthusiasm, intelligence, and her ability to live life. The intriguing, elderly woman mentioned she had a collectibles business. Not quite sure what that was, Melissa asked for clarification, and the business owner explained that she collected dolls, black artifacts and various items, and she also was doing substitute teaching.

Ms. Bridges gave her an envelope with a check for the amount of the repairs. Rather than just give her the check and leave, they sat and talked for hours. Though there was a 26-

year age difference, they had many things in common— from raising children to where their children lived and the activities they had participated in while growing up. Talking with her was surreal. She felt like the woman was one of her long-lost relatives who had breathed life into her bloodline. They sat in the cold car and just chatted and laughed.

She had two children and Melissa said, "So do I— a son and a daughter. Mrs. Bridges said, "Me too." Melissa did not find that unusual. It was just another thing they had in common. She said her daughter went to an Ivy League College, and Melissa asked, "Which one? because my daughter got accepted at an Ivy League School." The older woman shared the name, and Melissa commented that, of all the schools her daughter applied to, that was the school where she did not get accepted to.

Melissa then referenced the school her daughter had applied to, and Ms. Bridges said it was where her son-in-law attended law-school. They laughed when, again they found something else in common. When Ms. Bridges said her daughter lived in California, Melissa smiled. "So does my daughter!"

Melissa sought clarification of the California locale, since it was unfamiliar. Mrs. Bridges said her grandchildren attended private school, which did not sound odd. Melissa's children had many friends who attended private school— a new normal in middle-class black America. Melissa's son attended a private school for a year.

When Mrs. Bridges said her daughter was completing writing of the season finale episode for a popular TV show, Melissa's eyes widened. She could not believe it. She knew God had once again done something marvelous.

Mrs. Bridges continued to talk and gave Melissa her daughter's name, telling her to *google her*. Melissa's fingers could not move quickly enough. Her cell phone was not connecting, but Melissa continued to listen to Ms. Bridges talk and fiddled with it.

Melissa searched, and sure enough, her daughter was a TV writer for several shows and networks. Melissa was floored! She instantly said, "I need to speak with your daughter!" But Mrs. Bridges became strangely aloof. Melissa repeated herself. "I would like to talk with your daughter, if you do not mind."

The elderly, newly-found friend smiled and said, "Of course. I will reach out to her and let her know you will be calling." Melissa was in shock, because on Monday and Tuesday, she had written on a piece paper what God had directed her to do.

Melissa believed that the Holy Spirit had directed her to write names of television networks that may be interested in her research and then to write down that she should chat with a television producer or writer. Maybe, it was coming alive. Melissa was being obedient.

They chatted more, and Melissa smiled and said, "I cannot wait to tell your daughter how we met". Ms. Bridges abruptly stopped her and said, "Uh-unh. No, you will *not* be telling my daughter how we met."

Melissa looked her in the eyes and said that she understood. While smiling, she said, "I will not tell her we met up in a parking lot, and you handed me a check for $3,000". Ms. Bridges said, "No, you will not tell her any of this."

She said her daughter would fuss, and she didn't want to hear it. So, Melissa asked what she should say if the daughter asks how they met. The accident was in Southfield, so Ms. Bridges said, You could say we met in Southfield. You could say our meeting was an event and that we met by accident." All of which were true!

So they agreed if her daughter ever asked how they met, the response would be in Southfield at an event by accident.

Chapter 6

Destruction of a Routine

For I reckon that the sufferings of this present time [are]
not worthy [to be compared] with the glory which shall be
revealed in us. Romans 8:18

A Position Gone

In March of 2017, Melissa's employer told her that her position would be eliminated. she would lose her job after 14 years of service. The company would no longer require the services and contributions from her. They abruptly told her that her employment would end. She had worked with several leaders and had watched several people come and go. She had out-lasted many bosses, due to promotion, retirement, and even death.

She knew it was time for something different in her life. She wanted something that would get her excited and her look forward to coming to work. She had been restless in her mind and spirit, but she had not planned that the change would occur with a job elimination.

A part of her believed the elimination of her job was orchestrated by God. It was her way out. It was a clean break. She would never have quit the position on her own, unless she had another position lined up. Though she was ready to leave, and the position was no longer satisfying, it was not unbearable.

So she continued to stay, and she looked, applied, and interviewed for other positions. The issue was that the interviews did not quite fit. The job interviews did not convert to offers. So she stayed put and continued to pass the time away in the best way she knew how, which was by staying busy.

Her position was one that could have been defined as "a good job." That's what her momma would say. She served in a senior management position over a team of professionals. She was knowledgeable and comfortable with the work. People knew her and could call upon her for assistance. The elimination seemed very odd, since she had many years of experience in the field, had received outstanding evaluations, promotions, successes and was very competent in her role.

She had high expectations for herself and for the people who worked around her. She was the type of individual who would work hard and voice her opinion. Some would say she was a "strong Black woman," but she simply had strong work ethics and her team's results showed it.

They were very successful— so successful at times she knew it rubbed folks in the wrong manner. She knew her office had been a target from other areas within the institution. Though her area was very successful, some individuals questioned if there was duplication of tasks that she and her office performed.

Her fairly-new boss had come from a smaller institution and was getting grounded in his position. She sensed that he was persuaded and pressured by many, and she knew she did not rank as a favorite.

She was a part of the old regime, the very old regime. She had worked with 7 different bosses. She had the highest seniority of the leadership team, so she had observed the turnover of all the directors.

On the day that her boss shared the news, he indicated he was restructuring the organization in a way that would reflect the current climate. The office she worked in and its functions would not exist in the same manner.

Hearing this news, she was concerned about her team. *What would happen with them and their jobs?* Her boss answered, "Don't be concerned. Your entire team will be fine.

Their positions are not impacted by this new restructuring. Everyone is fine, except you."

Something seemed wrong with that statement. The unit would no longer exist, her position would be eliminated, and her people be transferred to other units. He was right! Everyone would be fine, but she thought even she would too. She just did not know how.

What she did know was that she was ready for a change, but not like this! She was being let go, but maybe she was being set free. The shock of the news did not permit her to think of her freedom though.

Over the last few months, she and her boss had been talking about filling positions in her area. He had asked her to write proposals to justify filling the positions. He even gave her feedback to have a stronger case for getting positions approved.

So the news did surprise her, because she had been led to expect that something else was going to happen. Had all the planning been in vain? Had the discussions and her efforts backfired in her face? She had supported several major initiatives, which brought in additional revenue— millions of dollars to the organization.

Generally, she was in the position where she advocated for others and now, she had to draw the courage to advocate for herself. She was faced with disappointment and fear, but she did not let fear win. She spoke up. She would have to gather strength from God and state her opinion.

She challenged him and asked questions about this decision. In her articulate, knowledgeable style, she asked, "Do you have a hidden agenda? What was your reasoning? When would this decision be effective?" When he remained silent, she guessed he was trying to be sympathetic or simply "on script."

He was unprepared to answer any of her questions, or he had decided he would answer very few of them, if any. He said her termination would happen in a month. She said, "No, this restructuring will not be effective on that date," and it was not. After all, she had contributed to the institution, she insisted, "You have to allow me to leave with grace and dignity."

What was she thinking? She insisted she had done too much for the organization for the action to be effective in a month. Again, she asked about his reasoning behind the decision, but he could not or would not tell her more.

Later in the meeting, with reference to her final day of employment, he said the final decision would have to go through leadership. It had to be announced to the entire organizational body before it would be finalized. There was nothing that sounded comforting or caring about his words.

The next governing meeting was scheduled in a month. She expected that for a decision of such magnitude—about someone who had contributed much, that they would have given it much more time. She deserved more than one month. *No, this decision would not be discussed in one month.* He listened to her and considered her words and agreed it would not be discussed in one month.

She was pleased she had the courage to speak up. They agreed that the decision would be discussed in five months, with an effective date four months later. Concerning this new timeline they had agreed upon, she was still unsure how he allowed her to stick around from the point of that meeting to nine months later.

No one did that. What was *he* thinking? What was she thinking? How humiliating it would be. It was early March, but now she would have to walk under the decision for nine months. She knew that God was with her.

A Long Walk...

A factual issue that she understood was that things had, in fact, changed, and the school's revenue was declining rapidly. The interest of students wanting to go into this field was not the top choice of students coming out of high schools. Nationally and locally, the numbers had declined steadily for several years. Her team had done several things to counter the declining interest, but numbers didn't lie. Enrollment numbers were declining.

This decline in enrollment was the beginning of the end and an indicator that it would be easy to justify the restructuring within the organization. After months of knowing that she would lose her job, the final day came. But before she left her job, it was a circus adventure.

For nine months, she walked through humiliation. The length of time that she worked, though providing for her financially, was lingering, challenging, demoralizing, and long. Yet through it all, it was a growth experience. Nevertheless, it was something she would never suggest for the employer or employee.

She would advise any employer that, if he/she makes a decision to eliminate an area director, the plug should be pulled right away. *Let the water drain quickly, rather than letting the water drip out slowly.* Staying around for too long is never good for anyone.

There she was, walking around for nine months, while the boss was unable to look her in the eyes unless he had to. Employees lost momentum, and it took every ounce of dignity for her to continue to go in (at least in the beginning). However, soon she realized that this was a gift.

Under the circumstances, she continued to get paid and grew stronger as a person. She sat through humiliating meetings, where the fate of her office and position was discussed right before her. She attended events where she witnessed people chatting about her fate.

She even developed the transition plan for the elimination of her office. She was pretty much on an island of discouragement and was digesting a pill that was larger and harder than anything she had ever swallowed. she quickly learned where her help came from.

Although she was down, *she was not crushed, perplexed, but not in despair* — *2 Corinthians 4:8.* She was blessed, and she knew it. God would carry her and would speak to her constantly. She started to hear HIM more clearly and in so many ways.

Her situation was interesting because she was still an active employee. In the midst of the turmoil, she realized that she had a special blessing. As an active employee, she was still eligible to take classes that that had already been purchased. Melissa was a student in the PhD program. Over the previous two years, she had been taking classes around the calendar to fulfill course requirements.

She was just at the point where she had completed all the course work, and the next part of fulfilling the PhD degree requirement was dissertation work. Dissertation work, research, and writing are extensive and tedious tasks that are done outside of the classroom and that require independent discipline and thinking to fulfill the degree requirement.

During the nine months waiting for her last day, she would begin this work with guidance from her committee chair... and an angel.

Chapter 7

The Holy Spirit Speaks

So do not fear, for I am with you; do not be dismayed, for I am your God. I will strengthen you and help you; I will uphold you with my righteous right hand. Isaiah 41:10

God's GOT This!

God had spoken plainly, and Melissa *had heard it many times. Psalms 62:11.* Melissa woke up around 4:00 a.m. awakened from sleep by the sounds of her voice. She heard her own voice speaking out loud, saying, "G-O-T." She heard herself saying, "G-O-T," and she then heard her reply to herself, saying, "Gift of Time." It was crazy and amazing all at the same time! *What was this?*

It was as if she eavesdropped on a conversation with herself— to herself, and she was listening to herself speak prophetically. She was intrigued and curious at the same time. She was half-asleep, but half-conscious— in a deep sleep— unable to physically shake herself completely awake, but she was awake enough so that she could hear herself.

It was odd... Again, she heard herself say, "G-O-T." She lay there, stuck in her deep rest, captured in quicksand and wrestling to break free and be awake. Puzzled, she replied to herself. "Gift of Time?" In that moment, she was in the presence of something.

It was something she could not describe, a feeling she could not shake. Listening to herself and not sure what it really meant, she soon heard it again, "G-O-T— Gift of Time. It was astounding and mysterious all at once. What did it mean? Was she just suppressing her daily life and encouraging herself in her dreams?

The phrase "G-O-T," a gift of time— is this what she had? Could she believe it and live it? Was it the spirit of God speaking? It was up to her to believe and take hold of it. She pondered the thought be depressed or live. She had been given a choice, a gift, a "gift of time." Eventually, Melissa dosed off to sleep and complete unconsciousness, back into a deep sleep.

A couple of hours later, she awoke to start her day. It was Wednesday, her day to workout at home before going to work. For three days a week, she worked out at home, and twice a week, she went to the gym to box. Tuesdays and Thursdays were more difficult. At 5 a.m., she practically threw herself from bed and stumbled to the bathroom, read a daily meditation and prepared to leave the house for the 10-minute drive.

It seemed robotic in action—not a lot of thinking, just preparing to leave and getting there. If she thought about it, she probably would not have gotten there. That day, however, was an easier day. She slept in until 6:00 a.m. and worked out at home.

She stumbled to the basement to get on the treadmill. When she ran on the treadmill, she watched TV to occupy her mind. However, on that morning, dragging a bit from the restless night and still not fully awake— she had awoken earlier to the G-O-T phrase— She ran slowly on the treadmill and watched television to jumpstart her workout.

Typically, she watched something she had recorded on the DVR. She enjoyed getting caught up on various television shows and not being interrupted. Her husband was always asleep at that hour, and it was a perfect time for herself, with no interruptions.

What would she watch that morning *Have and Have Nots* or *Murder, She Wrote* or *Queen Sugar* or *Joel Osteen*? Would it be laughter, drama, suspense or spiritual to begin her day. It just depended on how she was feeling and what she needed to get her day started. On that day, since she did not read a scripture for morning meditation, nor prayed, she decided to watch Joel Osteen.

After all, it was important to feed her spirit early and let God direct her path. So on that day, it was Joel for the run. After his morning joke and while she was gearing up to run, he started with the theme of his message of God's "Got" this. *Interesting theme*, she thought, *God's got this.* She listened more intensely and thought, *God's got WHAT?* and then it hit her...*G-O-T!*

Was it a coincidence, happenstance, or luck? *God's got this.* Joel then clarified by saying, "Are you dealing with children who are acting unlike you never imagined they could? (she responded, *yes*). Then Joel said, *"God's Got this."* And he said something along the lines, "Are things and people strange on your job?" (she responded, *absolutely yes!*) He repeated, *"God's got this."*

He said other things, but by then her curiosity was peaked. She was all-in, awake and RUNNING. A sign! She realized that the message was for her, and it was no coincidence. God was speaking directly to her!

She had begun running at a higher pace on the treadmill and listening, because she knew that yet again, God was communicating with her. She realized that God had given her an introduction to a conversation through herself, to herself, through her dreams. Joel affirmed the code of "G-O-T."

It was complex, and yet simple. God's Got this situation, and she had a gift of time. Essentially, the message was telling her not to be afraid, that though things were confusing to her, God ultimately had her in the palm of His hands. God had given her a gift of time.

She realized that God had her back. *God's got this. Don't worry!* Yes, on that Wednesday, in the early hours of the morning— from a pre-recorded show, Joel was a conduit. He was prophetic. He was speaking to her, and she contemplated if she would accept the sign and appreciate the wonder? It was manna for the day while she was in the valley.

God speaks to us, through others and through us. He gives us thoughts and signs, but often we overlook them and ignore the happenstances. However, on that morning, she heard and recognized the sign. God used Joel as a second voice.

The first voice was Melissa's own— the Holy Spirit spoke *through* her. In Joel's message, he told Melissa how to handle her situation. First, He told her to stop wondering about what would be next and worrying how things would turn out. Things would work out. God had a solution. Second, Joel shared how God had the situation under control. It was no surprise to Him.

The morning activity was all so mesmerizing. She had a prelude to the conversation at 4 a.m., and Joel's message comforted her with God's message. God told her to be calm. He told her that it was a matter of time, and that she needed to live in peace and keep her joy.

God shared that **what was meant for her harm would be used for her good.** — **Genesis 50:20.** Yes, God had given her a gift of time, but it was for an assignment. God was preparing her for His greater need. The question was, *would she trust, believe and be patient?*

She believed the message and could visualize a new and different lifestyle. She was able to imagine bigger things for her life than the job that she was losing. She had an assignment. She began to dream bolder dreams for herself.

He told her to remain in the faith, to work diligently at completing her PhD research. Yes, it was humiliating and a hard situation. However, she had received a gift of time. Many had much more difficult challenges. God had her back. She did not have to worry or be discouraged. She only had to be open to how God would guide her life. She had to trust!

She continued going to work in an uncomfortable and unexplainable situation. She was growing more confident in the valley. While being in the valley and still going to work, she began smiling, greeting people and working arduously at her research.

She remembered what Joel said, "God's got this." Things happen in God's will. The situation was no surprise to God. He allowed things to happen in order to show that *He is God*, an amazing God. He would get the glory. Surely, it was an experience that God had under His control.

Through this valley experience, Melissa received manna and signs from God. Her job was to trust, believe and stay connected to the source. God provides signs in the oddest ways. Her job was to *wait patiently and confidently (Romans 8:25)*, to believe it.

God not only wanted her to believe in His power, but God wanted her to experience His glory and His favor. God wanted her to trust Him. God was going to make a way where she could not see a way. She had to stay in faith, trust, believe and continue to work. She needed to surrender to worry, *Let Go and Let God*. Trust, research and write!

The Count of Monte Cristo

God speaks again. She was at the beautiful historic Congregational Church that was designed by black architects. The church represented 100 years of leadership, vision, courage and spirituality. The church had a rich history, a strong social justice presence, and a welcoming congregation.

Melissa, along with her family, had attended the congregational church for over 25 years. Sitting in the fourth row and listening attentively. She knew on that day, Reverend Jewell would have a message for her. The reverend was a dynamic and passionate African American preacher with a strong delivery. She had a passion for God that was infectious.

Members from the congregation had commented earlier that when the reverend spoke, they instantly could tell she had a special relationship with the Heavenly Father and she boldly trusted Him. They said Reverend Jewell could interpret the word of God in a relatable manner that was invigorating.

That morning, as Melissa sat meditating and being in the presence of God, she asked God to send her a message. *Please speak to me!* The choir finished praise and worship and Reverend Jewell began her message.

With a sprinting walk, she quickly moved from the pulpit and stood in the center of the congregation. She raised her hand and asked, by a sign of raised hands, who has seen the movie, *The Count of Monte Cristo*? Many persons raised their hands.

Melissa had not watched the movie, but she was intrigued to hear more. Reverend Jewell used an analogy from the movie, a spiritual metaphor. And wouldn't you know it, God began speaking and had a message for her.

The movie was more than a metaphor. God spoke directly to her. For this spiritual metaphor, Reverend Jewell highlighted how the movie contained many real-life elements: naivety, jealousy, envy, trust, betrayal, denial and revenge— all the things that made a good drama. *All the congregation needed was popcorn!* She listened intently to hear how the climax of the movie included Jesus.

Edmond was betrayed by his friend due to jealousy and competitiveness. His friends and the people in his inner circle ceased being supportive or loyal toward him. He was being treated differently and was framed. It was unfair and did not make sense. Yet through it all, Edmond maintained hope about what was going on.

He assumed everything would be all right because he was innocent. But no, Edmond was sent to prison. He had been betrayed by the very people that he supported and trusted. Edmond was in the valley. While broken in prison and alone for several years, he met a fellow inmate—someone he could trust, a friend who told him, "Let neglect become your ally."

The "brokenness" and loneliness were a gift. What does one do with silence and time? One works towards a goal. Edmond met his goal. His life did change forever. Melissa heard that message, a message that resonated with her.

She was often in a position of being alone, in a valley. No longer was she being invited to meetings and asked for her opinion or contributions. Reverend Jewell's message was for her. God was speaking. *Don't waste energy on anger. Use that energy constructively and positively. What is your goal?*

What she interpreted from the message was that God wanted her to take advantage of her time of isolation. *Use the isolation and neglect for good. Let rejection become an ally. Let rejection allow a change in direction and provide a gift of time.* She thought *well, okay, let's do this! Continue to research and write!*

The movie was a sign. God had used the associate pastor's sermon to speak to Melissa. On that day, God didn't speak as he did in the Old Testament, but rather through a dynamic, feisty, female preacher and a movie. As the service ended, Melissa was at peace and at a place where she could recognize His voice. She had a relationship with God. They communicated through music, television, movies, reading materials and people. She thought to herself, *I will look back and say how I got over?*

It shall be when these signs come to you, do for yourself what the occasion requires, for God is with you. 1 Samuel 10:7 Neither height nor depth, nor anything else in all creation, will be able to separate us from the love of God in Christ Jesus our Lord — Romans 8:39

Chapter 8

You Must Believe and Work

Whatever you do, work heartily, as for the Lord and not for men — Colossians 3:23

Time to Get Busy

She let go of her pride and put her faith to work. So rather than being depressed about her position being eliminated and pointing out what was unfair, she enthusiastically went to a job that was providing her with freedom. She enthusiastically went to work, knowing that she was given a gift of time.

For the course of nine months, after she completed any work tasks, she diligently worked on her PhD research. She read articles, perused the isles and shelves at the campus library, got books and wrote her literature review. The routine became therapeutic, enduring from March through December, until her very last day on the job.

During that nine-month period, she continued to provide guidance to her team when it was needed, she wrote a transitional plan to eliminate her department, and she met with her supervisor to provide any updates. She knew she was there to work, and she worked diligently, and it was up to the company to utilize her, but work got done. She decided to let neglect become her ally. She took possession of "a gift of time."

During the nine months, there were rumors about her job being eliminated. Yet she was not distracted. She occasionally attended meetings to which she hadn't been invited, partially for fear of a law suit. She listened to how they would eliminate her office and her position.

In that time, she got a tougher skin and became resilient. She even sat through one meeting where he told her team, "Don't worry, you'll be fine. Only Melissa will be hurt by this." He said it in a matter-of-fact manner—five times to be exact, throughout the meeting.

He was attempting to comfort them. "Don't worry, you'll be fine. Only she'll be hurt by this." "Don't worry, you'll be fine. Only she'll be hurt by this." "Don't worry, you'll be fine. Only she'll be hurt by this." She sat counting, marking on a piece of paper each time he stated it. "Don't worry, you'll be fine. Only she'll be hurt by this."

He actually thought his approach was okay. Apparently, he thought he was doing the right thing by consoling the group. On the other hand, she thought, *Who does this?* Each person from the team seemed puzzled and bewildered about the insensitive statement.

She thought it was humiliating and again began to question her God. *What had she done?* It was crazy, but she left the meeting, held her head high and held firm to the message from Reverend Jewell's sermon. *Let neglect become your ally.*

Research and writing became her focus, and she disregarded uncomfortable moments. She also knew the scripture said, **God is just: He will pay back trouble to those who trouble you — 2 Thessalonians 1:6.** She reached to the scriptures to keep her strength. **Thou preparest a table for me in the presence of my enemies — Psalms 23:5.**

She knew God was probably speaking to her, *prior* to the elimination decision. She was just too occupied in her own head and world with so many activities. Being a wife, a mother, a professional, a student, a servant at church, an organization member, a friend and a person who worked-out, and going to various events kept her more than busy.

She was all over the place… and no place at the same time. She had become so occupied with so many worldly things that God was barely in the equation, so she didn't recognize the cues, even though they were right before her. God had been talking, but she had allowed His voice to be diluted.

Life activities and other priorities had weakened her relationship with Him. It was her choosing. She thought her life was full, she thought it was complete. The many things that occupied her had weakened her relationship with God.

It was during this elimination period, when her world came crashing to a halt, that she began to hear God again. She imagined He said, *Can you hear me now?* She began noticing everything that was going on around her, during the day, in the evening, at night and even in the dew hours of the morning. God was speaking.

She reflected on her daily life and knew she had way too much going on. Even though she had given God a bit of "toothbrush time" in the morning—a fraction of time to read a meditation or attend a church service, she surely wasn't developing a nurturing ongoing relationship. She had not been investing time in her Godly relationship, but rather she functioned in a manner where she could do all things all the time. *Well, that recipe did not last long!*

Chapter 9

As for man, his days are like grass; As a flower of the field, so he flourishes. When the wind has passed over it, it is no more, And, its place acknowledges it no longer —
Psalms 103: 15-16

Seasons

The conclusion of her nine months was fast-approaching. She continued to go to work until her last day. In her last days, she experienced the seasons of Michigan from her office window, the amazing work of God. All four seasons of the Midwest revealed their dazzling candor, from March through December.

She was fortunate to have an office with a tremendous view. Her sixth-floor office had a couple more windows than the typical offices which provided an extraordinary view of the sprawling, hilly and picturesque campus. She saw and appreciated things that she never paid much attention to earlier.

The right-side window of her desk displayed the beauty of God's craftmanship. She had a live canvas of artwork that bestowed the magnificent details of the seasons. She noticed the live, three-dimensional artwork that was in her view, right outside of her window.

No longer included in meetings and no longer running around the building to assist people, she began to appreciate the enhanced beauty of nature. Despite not being able to burn off the extra calories from moving about the building and campus, it was a splendid picture of nature.

She spent most of her time situated in her office, after doing her work, focusing on course work, gazing out of the window and exploring the contents of her mind. The gift of time and gift of being in her perfectly situated office was peaceful. She just had to make sure to get up and take breaks and walk around the building to burn some calories.

It was a small thing, but in the middle of that difficult period, she had an opportunity to reflect and surround herself with pure Michigan nature. She could see the well-manicured, groomed grounds of the campus, the hills of plush green grass where deer pranced in postured formation or lay around in relaxation.

The trees abundantly situated across the grounds were Oaks, Red Maples, Eastern Hemlocks, Black Maples, Black Gums, European Beech and Evergreens. They were strategically planted to showcase a hilly, inviting lawn where children ran and played across the landscape. She heard the inspirational sounds of carefree living.

A childcare facility situated nearby provided the joys of innocence. Throughout the day and when the weather permitted, the children played outside. She listened to the blissful laughter and screams of innocent play from three-and four-year-old kids. They ran through the grass, played in the fun house and slid down the slides. Their sounds were radiant and exhilarating, sounds that brought solace each day and all day during the nine months.

She noticed how she truly appreciated the beauty of life, trees and flowers outside of her window. For the time, she embraced the moments and did not dwell on potential problems, but rather she focused on the moments of nature. *On the glorious splendor of your majesty, and on your wondrous works, I will meditate — Psalm 125:5*

Midwest weather had a way of being unpredictable. In the completion of winter and the birth of spring, March and April were months where people hoped for warmer weather, but winter still held on tight to prove it had the last word—its final proof of strength before spring burst through. Inexperienced Midwesterners might contemplate a hope that winter was over, but they always knew that there were still possible snowstorms to validate that winter still lingered and had the upper hand. The trees still had frost on the branches and a winter coat still was required. *He has made everything beautiful in its time. — Ecclesiastes 3:11.* Late April and May brought the birth of something new, something fresh, something to anticipate. Everything began sprouting. She noticed the season of spring miraculously transform from winter. The sky shifted from gray to an uplifting soft baby blue, and different shades of blue—royal blue and light blue, with white fluffy clouds lying against the backdrop.

The grass was growing rapidly green, and when it was newly cut, the smell of earthy freshness permeated the air. The trees stood strong and firm, reaching toward the sun after enduring the lingering cold, harsh winter. The branches displayed speckles of pastels and white buds. They were budding and blossoming; there were shades of a pretty pink, light lavender, pale green and lime green.

The tulips and daffodils were radiating a warm inviting scent. There was hope for a new future, with hard winter behind. The birds, chirping with song, had returned and were flying across the skies. Children blissfully chatted at higher levels of excitement. The campus was pregnant with new life.

Then came summer, June through August. Nature had given birth. The sky was at its peak of Egyptian and sapphire blue, with white clouds standing in formation. The sun was smiling and beaming in its brightest form. The landscape was splendid.

The plentiful trees, fully sprouted with leaves, were waving with joy as the wind passed through with delight. The live canvas took on an appearance of joy, strength and courage. Nature had survived the rough winter, barely remembering its brutal effects.

The trees were luscious with green leaves, leaves in a rich variety of colors and shapes. The colors of forest green, hunter green and fern green were dancing upon the branches.

The children were in their designated area, running, playing and engaging with one another as birds flew around in majestic patterns. she saw different areas of the live canvas—a family of deer, prancing with confidence, male deer, walking in long strides, two or more following casually and nibbling in the grass.

Farther out, she saw more herds of deer—baby fawns, freshly-born to their mothers, skipping with new independence and strutting playfully across the lawn with the wonderment of a new environment.

Next in sequence was fall, September through November. The window canvas changed into a masterpiece of flamboyant colors. It was art in motion. The colors of the leaves were extravagant; they changed to orange, blazing red, golden yellow and burnt burgundy. The trees displayed different shapes of leaves and majestic colors.

The sun was beaming and reflecting on the leaves and grass. It was an orchestrated symphony of color. The sky still showed hints of blue had a laziness about it. The white clouds were sitting in calmness. There was a crispness in the air that signaled a change that was coming.

The leaves were slowly settling into their winter places on lawns, as fall was being ushered onto the campus. The sounds of children laughing then included the rustling in the fallen leaves. The warmth faded. Soon, God would breathe down and the leaves would dissipate. Sweaters and light jackets would enter the campus.

The grass withers, the flowers fades but the word of our God will stand forever — Isaiah 40:8. It was mid-December. On that day, when she walked into her office and looked out the window, she immediately noticed the view was different.

The campus was quiet, no longer vibrant with life. The leaves were gone; the tree trunks and branches were noticeably different. The trees were bare. On the ground lay brown lifeless leaves that would return to the earth. The plentiful deciduous trees, surrounded by tall evergreens, stood naked, shivering in the breeze.

The sky, no longer blue, appeared gray and hazy. The energy and power of life, as she had seen it and experienced it, was gone. The campus seasons spring, summer, and fall had passed, and then she reflected on the seasons, as they represented her time at the institution.

Winter had arrived. Her time working at the campus had become dormant. Spring, summer and fall, in their beauty, had passed — as had her time there. *God had made everything beautiful for its own time — Ecclesiastes 3:11.*

It was time to depart, and she knew it. She completed nearly 14 years of work at that university, worked with seven different bosses, worked with a passionate intelligent team and had served with excellence. She completed her time with outstanding evaluations, two promotions and many accomplishments.

God had closed that door, and there was no forcing it to re-open. She had enjoyed many seasons and had contributed her talent and skills. But now it was time to depart. Her seasons were up!

He said to them, 'It is not for you to know times or seasons that the Father has fixed by his own authority — Acts 1:7.

Chapter 10

A Harvest
Your beginnings will seem humble, so prosperous will your future be — Job 8:7

A New Road to a PhD

A new routine, a different view, an exciting experience. Melissa was embracing and trusting HIM. January 2018 marked the start of an auspicious new year—a new opportunity, a re-start, re-boot. It was as if, in completing this work, she had boarded a flight on a North American X-14 aircraft, heading to another time zone.

With butterflies in her stomach, she boarded, strapped in, traveling down the runway, bracing herself as she ascended with anticipation. Her eyes open, the jet rushed at maximum speed to break the bonds of Earth to level on a higher plane. The trip destination was completion of a PhD.

The process of completing the tasks was handwringing, daunting, exhilarating, and yet therapeutic. She progressed with her research in a swift manner, with intent and speed. During the previous year, while she was still going to work, her PhD committee chair met with her weekly for progress updates.

Chair SS was an angel, sent to be Melissa's guide. SS, who had a matter-of-fact style that was quantifiable in nature, would get her to the Promised Land. She had asked herself, *Did you complete the task, or not? Were you putting in the time?* SS was a "pro" at completing the PhD process and knew the special recipe of the formula. She would motivate Melissa and keep her over-drive personality intact with deadlines of work to be done.

SS knew after the class phase of obtaining a PhD, the candidate had to have the structure and discipline to complete the work. It was important to develop a routine, a structure of accountability. During the nine-month period, while she was still working, Melissa had mastered that routine. As she entered this new phase, she knew she would no longer be going to an office every day, where the structure of the workday provided accountability.

Reflecting on the past, she believed God knew exactly what she needed to get through the elimination period, and SS was sent to keep her accountable. So HE aligned the timing so she could be counseled by a PhD chair during that delicate time. She had developed a routine of writing that she continued to follow.

SS was supportive of all her students. She was attuned to the business of completion and used a quantifiable approach to get there. What impressed many students was that SS was acutely responsive to her students. A student could email the chair materials in the middle of the night, day or afternoon, and somehow, she had the ability to respond within hours.

Many PhD students benefitted from her support. She was a dedicated soul who took care of business. Melissa could have chosen several people to be her chair, but for the task of that journey, she needed a well-experienced and seasoned committee chair, who fully understood the tortuous path of obtaining a PhD.

After her job ended, she worked on her PhD research and writing mostly at the neighborhood public library. When she did not feel like leaving the house, she worked in her home, and when the weather turned to a summer sensation, she worked at the park. She called it her "multi-office locations."

The public library was the "West Office," as it was west of her home. Her home was the "Central Office," where she worked in a quiet room, and then there was the "Lake Office," where she went to the park.

During the winter months, while at the West Office, she gazed out the window at a big oak tree that had witnessed years over many decades. The tree had the height and gnarled crevices of several generations. Its roots were deep and wide to support the dignity of its stature.

As she sat in the office, the stillness of winter engulfed her mind when she gazed for too long. She found herself pondering thoughts about her career, and she eventually was guided back to her writing. The Central Office, where Melissa often wrote, provided a comfortable home environment. Her office had a tremendous view of both sides of her home, to the right of her desk, in the spring, she could see the backyard, where a large Sugar Maple tree with branches extended across the grass with fresh new leaves.

To the left, she could see out the large picturesque atrium windows and see the finely manicured lawns and landscaping of the houses in her suburban neighborhood. And then, there was the Lake office at Kensington Park. The Lake office coddled her with trees, walking geese and calming water. Melissa was immersed in the elements of nature. The view was spectacular.

Once arriving to the Lake Office, she dragged a picnic table across the grass and strategically placed it in front of the lake and under a large oak tree to get the right amount of shade and a lake view. During the day, the Lake Office provided a serene atmosphere, as typically, there were not many people around, and she could commune with God.

The routine was mundane: Each day, after a morning workout, she arrived with an overstuffed backpack, with files of materials, articles and reference books. She arrived early at a designated office, pulled out her brown teddy bear, a tiny rock with the words of Einstein—*In the midst of every difficulty lies an opportunity,"* a scripture in her heart and her material.

The articles were about spirituality, about black women who were leaders, about self-determination along with several reference books. The topic and materials were very much associated with who she was and what interested her: black women who were determined, spirituality and leaders.

The items would be methodically and tactically placed on a table surrounding her materials so that when she needed inspiration, she would look up and glance at one of the items. The bear from the African American Museum symbolized the struggle of many people and her ancestors who came before her.

She purchased it while visiting the National Museum of African American History in D.C. She loved museums and reflecting on the lives of those who persevered through unspeakable obstacles and conquered many challenges. It reminded her of people, who had a struggle that was much more about overpowering in life experiences than she had known or would ever know.

Each day, she a woman driven by achievement, would check off the accomplished tasks from her checklist. She completed the task of completing each segment of research, inspired by the findings, encouraged by the hope, and motivated to finish her work.

She trusted in a higher being to lead her in the endeavor to complete a task that was much bigger than she imagined. Excited, she watched how God cleared paths for her to complete steps and intercepted plays that would slow her down. God was in charge of her daily playbook and was her coach.

She was simply a player, running and executing plays and calls. Even when she got off course by applying and interviewing for positions, God would tilt her back to the course designed for her path at that specific time. Thus obtaining a job at that time was not what God had destined for her, not yet anyway.

If it was not a part of the PhD journey, then those seeds seemed not to settle on fertile soil, the effort would not come to fruition. How frustrating it was when she used energy to search for positions, and then, the opportunity did not work out as she thought it would.

In her mind, she wanted to depart from the course of researching, collecting data, coding and writing in order to return to a familiar routine of going to a job, but that was not the plan that God had for her. Each job interview—and there were several—did not result in her starting in a new position. Often, she was a finalist, but something prevented the closing of the deal. So she pivoted from that effort to the plan of completing the PhD It had to be God's plan, because that is where God showed up.

God showed up for the completion of the Institution Review Board application submission. It was a required step, an application of many pages to provide evidence of what her research entailed and then the hope the university overseers would give approval to conduct research.

She recalled going to a workshop that introduced what it would entail. She left the workshop intimidated and mystified, but she had to simply trust, surrender and do the work. It was a step-by-step process.

God was there as she completed the pages, and she expeditiously executed the process in record time so that she got approval without the normal mundane protocol steps of providing additional verification. It was an intimidating process that she was grateful to avoid. Her defense chair was incredibly skilled, keeping her progressing and encouraged, moving forward and believing she could accomplish her objective.

Then there was the concern she had about identifying the participants for her research. Where would she find the people? The participants she needed were anomalies—they were black women who were top executive, senior-level leaders in higher education or hospitals. They were sprinkled across a vast country.

How would she find these women and interview them? Would they be willing to be interviewed? Would they be receptive to being included for this research topic? She was hopeful for identifying and finding an acceptable number of women.

In the morning, O LORD, You will hear my voice; In the morning I will order my prayer to You and eagerly watch —
Psalm 5:3

She had returned home and was sitting in her home office. It was early in the morning, after a 6:00 a.m. boxing class. She sat, thought, prayed and prepared for the day. She knew that it was in the mornings that she heard God the most loudly.

She sat amid her thoughts and honored God. She prayed, read scripture and meditated. It was her way of communicating with God. She knew He would speak, as he had spoken many times before. Typically, she would have many thoughts, and this morning was no different. He would tell her to prepare for her interviews.

This subject of the dissertation concerned her most, since she knew that it would not be easy to identify the women. If she could not identify the women, then she would not be able to gather the data to study the research. She had heard about this nightmare from a gentleman who could not obtain the data he needed to do his research, which extended his dissertation writing for an additional year. She did not have an extra year. The concern secretly haunted her.

On that morning, as she sat quietly in her Central Office, she heard the Holy Spirit speak—not audibly, but in her mind and spirit. He told her that, since she would be traveling out of state for a visit, she should plan to interview some women for her research.

She was shocked to hear this message, as she had not confirmed anyone to be interviewed. Initially, she ignored the thought, but the thought kept nagging at her. Finally, she got on her computer and googled universities and reviewed their executive team members who were located in the cities where she would travel.

What amazed her was that, when she looked at the senior executive leadership team at the first university she researched, she immediately saw a black woman who fit the criteria for her research. It was odd! She even chuckled. *Okay, God, so was my search a lucky guess or am I being guided?* She momentarily contemplated and finally decided she would call the executive leader's assistant—the person who handles the executive's calendar.

She would be the logical person to contact, since Melissa knew she was the person who managed the executive's calendar. It was early in the morning, close to 8 a.m. *She should be in.* So Melissa assumed the secretary would answer the phone and she would explain the reason for her call—that she was doing research, would be in town, and wondered if she could have 45 minutes of the Vice President's time.

Melissa would use the language from her prepared IRB script. She had no idea if the plan would work, but she was going to courageously give it a shot. She chose to believe. God was directing her.

She mustered enough boldness and made the call. All prepared, she dialed the phone, but the secretary did not answer. Shockingly, the actual Vice President answered. *Oh boy!* That was not expected. Melissa had prepared for the secretary. The executive was not supposed to answer the phone.

She had called the general office number, so immediately she changed her script to address the Vice President and proceeded with her request. She introduced herself and explained the intent of her call. The Vice President explained in a welcoming voice, that generally she did not answer that phone line, but her assistant had not yet arrived at work.

After taking a deep breath, Melissa explained the focus of her research and asked if she could get on her calendar for an interview. She heard, "Yes. Please email my secretary, and she will place you on my calendar."

Once again, Melissa pondered and asked, *Wow, what just happened? Was this God?*

She sat in amazement. Did the conversation actually happen? How could it be? God gave her a word. She chose to believe and responded, based on the word given to her. Being prepared, she diligently persevered toward the goal. When she showed up, God met her and helped her.

Without hesitation, she praised her heavenly Father, for she knew that this was the work of the Lord. *His eye is on the Sparrow, and He watches M e— Matthew 6:26.* She reflected and thought about the series of events that occurred that morning.

It was more than coincidental that the very first institution she researched in a city that she had not considered contained an individual who fit her research criteria, and when she called, the Vice President answered the phone and agreed to be interviewed. *Nothing but God!*

She repeated the exercise again. She researched and identified another institution that fit the criteria of her research. She reviewed the executive team, carefully checking to see if a black woman was in one of the top executive rank positions. *B-I-N-G-O!* She had found another! *Well*, she thought, *that's all I need.*

She repeated the steps and phoned the assistant. That time, the assistant *did* answer, but the outcome did not turn out like the first call. She would have to do more work, explain more and be more patient. That time, the endeavor of getting an interview would take a week. She had to send an email explaining the research, and she had to wait until the Vice President reviewed the email request and responded.

She copied the secretary on the request to the Vice President, which was intentional because Melissa knew it would then be easier to reach out to the secretary again. After a week passed, a determined Melissa contacted the secretary to see if the Vice President's calendar might accommodate her when she was in town.

After a week of patience and persistence, the Vice President agreed. Melissa proceeded in this manner, gathering names of possible interviews and requesting referrals during interviews. It eventually paid off, and she acquired nearly double the designated number of women needed for her research. *Won't He Do It!*

She had acquired enough data to do coding, analysis and interpretation. It would take months to conduct the tasks of analysis, listening to recordings, reading and re-reading and re-rereading transcripts, note-taking, coding and interpretation. It was a churning process that would be well worth the effort. She was finally ready to begin writing.

I am sending an angel ahead of you to guard you along the way and to bring you to the place I have prepared — Exodus 23:20

Chapter writing was hard! Writing was not her strength. She would much rather talk, eat, watch television or anything else other than sit down and write. Was she smart enough? Did she have what it took? All those thoughts that were placed in her mind to prevent her from the task.

But GOD deployed another angel. She arrived early in the process. It was a person who would walk with her along the way throughout the PhD journey. The angel was a super grammarian! She knew grammar and the rules of writing. She was old-school—she understood grammar rules that educators do not teach anymore.

The angel worked with her during the calendar year. She came with books and actual lesson plans. She taught and tutored Melissa. She helped Melissa address oral and written communication deficiencies. All Melissa could think was, *What kind of God is this?* He sent exactly what she needed.

Once she surrendered and got out of the way, God provided her with what and whom she needed to complete the task and destination that HE had at hand for her. Edit after edit, redo after redo, and chapter after chapter, the angel was there to encourage, suggest ideas and guide her.

She worked day and evening, but she did not tire of the routine or fear the task. God was with her and gave her energy, strength and angels.

The Ninth Month

***Be strong and** do not give up, **for your work will be rewarded** —2 Chronicles 15:7*

During the month of August, she was on cruise-control as she continued to write her last chapters. She was working at the Lake Office on a regular basis at a steady pace. The Lake Office was an exhilarating office, as the breeze hugged her face, and she typed word after word. Each day, she captured additional insights from her participants as she reassessed transcripts and re-analyzed data.

Chapter by chapter, she submitted each one to her chair, who reviewed the work and provided feedback. Frequently, she had to make edits to give her writing a more scholarly tone, or she had to explain content to the satisfaction of her chair.

Like pregnancy—after a while, the excitement was gone, and she just wanted to be finished. At times, she became frustrated, but she knew it was only because the journey was coming to an end. She likened that part of the writing process to being pregnant. She thought it was similar to the feelings of wanting to be finished and *just have the baby!*

In her mind, she imagined it was her ninth month—she was overweight, not sleeping regularly, antsy, and there were quickening labor pains. So when the chair red-lined or questioned three-quarters of her chapter—after complaining about a passage, it was okay. That was normal. Soon, the baby would arrive. She wanted a healthy baby, so she had to do the edits and jump through the hoops.

The chapters were coming together. Each approved chapter was a step getting closer to "pre-defense." It was a sure sign that she was arriving at her destiny. Pre-defense involved her having to go before her committee, and they would drill her intensely on each chapter to determine if there were flaws in her work and check to determine if she was completely knowledgeable on specific topics. At the end of the final chapter, when approval was given, the chair indicated it was time to schedule the pre-defense.

It's Getting Real

The time is near when all things will end. So, think clearly and control yourselves so you will be able to pray — 1 Peter 4:7

When the day of pre-defense came, she was prepared. She awakened early that morning, and all her materials were ready. She had her backpack, loaded with a binder, articles, transcripts and any other items that would support her in referencing her writings.

She thought it would be good to record the pre-defense meeting, so she packed a small audio recorder as well. She didn't want her nerves to cause her to miss out on hearing any important information. She wanted to capture everything. It was her first pre-defense, so she didn't really know how to properly prepare or what to expect.

As they sat in a large conference room, she spread her materials around her. She had her pad of paper for taking proper notes for each chapter and her audio recorder to the right of her to pick up each question.

The committee sat before her and had their materials strategically laid out. They began with pleasantries and then began to drill down on each chapter. She answered directly and supported her thinking and logic. She intensely took notes as they went through the process. Pre-defense went very well! There were several questions, lots of answers, minimal changes and a date scheduled to defend.

For he says, "In the time of my favor I heard you, and in the day of salvation I helped you." I tell you, now is the time of God's favor, now is the day of salvation — 2 Corinthians 6:2

Defense Day, October 9, 2018. She could not believe the day had arrived! She had brought her idea to life, with God. The many hours of research, the time sitting in the library and the long evenings had come to closure. Though some would say the process was not that long, it was all she thought about and worked on since hearing about her job being eliminated.

Every place she went, it seemed to always come back to her research and what she was doing. She felt nervous, but more than anything, she felt gratitude. She knew God had walked with her and provided her the resources for the journey.

Not neglecting to meet together, as is the habit of some, but encouraging one another, and all the more as you see the Day drawing near — Hebrews 10:25

The room was full! People were everywhere. All the chairs were full. There was standing room only. Wow! Where did all the people come from? This journey of four-plus years (especially the last year) yielded relationships and friends from various places.

The attendees came from out-of-state, locally, from the university and from the church. Her village had expanded, with many teammates. All she could think while defending her research was, *What kind of God is this?* How had she gotten there?

Research had been completed, chapters written, pre-defense passed and now the official formal test—defense. Yes, the day arrived. She had overcome each hurdle. She ran the race. God carried her. She was prepared. She knew this research material.

She had lived and breathed that phenomenon of faith, spirituality and self-determination. Though she heard many stories of faith, it was her story that had been written and was being told. Melissa, a child of God, was being guided to a destination through which she had to move with trust. She could only *defeat the challenges of this journey because she believed that Jesus is the Son of God* —*1 John 5:5*

Chapter 11

Staying Connected to the Source

*I am the vine, and you are branches. Those who remain
in me, and I in them, will bear much fruit; for you can do
nothing without me. — John 15:5*

Another Year

Her 54th birthday was in November. She smiled to herself
as she turned 54 in Paris, with her husband and children. A
year earlier, she had not imagined she would be in Paris for
her birthday. She was way too busy to plan the trip.

Again, she credited God for the trip, because it was an act
of God that got her to travel at that point in time. In the human
flesh, she did not think it was possible, given her financial
state—plus she had been way too busy with her research.

The time needed to complete her PhD required much from
her. In addition to the energy of the PhD research, she had to
be conservative with her spending, and given that she was not
working and had not worked for over a year, she was not
planning an extravagant vacation.

But God, *What's impossible for man is possible with God.
— Luke 18:27,* would place a situation in front of her that she
could not refuse, and it would be a gift for completing her
PhD—plus a special bonus gift.

Simone! Melissa's German exchange student from 16
years ago was getting married, and her fiancé had reached out
to Melissa to request that the family attend. She hesitated and
pondered why would they take on such an expense at that
time. What would it cost? How could she justify it?

Once she surrendered and did not worry, concerning
thoughts of the costs, everything then fell into place. And

several months later, there she was in Paris, so for the time she enjoyed a two-week trip in Europe with her family.

She had traveled to Germany in Munich and the Bavarian Alps then to Vienna, and then to Paris. The trip was exhilarating. They visited numerous museums and monumental sites. She was in Europe because of Simone's marriage. Melissa and Marc, Simone's finance, had planned the family's surprise visit for the wedding—it would be so special.

They sent emails back and forth for an entire year, discussing the arrangements. It was exhilarating to plan the trip as Simone's gift, and the trip would be a birthday gift for Melissa and a PhD gift as well. *Wow! Look at God! Three gifts in one!*

After the long flight, the family was exhausted, since they had been traveling for over nine hours, but they all found a second wind with the anticipation of Simone answering the knock at the door. So when they arrived early Wednesday morning at Simone's doorstep, it felt wonderful that they pulled off the surprise.

Simone was shocked! Jasper rang the doorbell. When Simone opened the door, her eyes widened as she recognized him instantly, and immediately she stopped in her tracks. She gasped for air, let out a squeal, covered her face and smiled as she realized her American family was in Germany.

Jasper was first in line. She hugged him and rubbed his back. It was a thing that she always did to show affection. Each family member then proceeded to greet her with a smile and hug. She had not seen them for over 15 years. Jasper and Lola were six and nine years old the last time she saw them. Now they were 22 and 25.

Love is Love

The wedding took place in the Bavarian Alps in a log cabin. Simone and Marc met in the Bavarian Alps on a snowboarding trip. It was such a beautiful, scenic place—mountain tops and small towns. The drive to get there from Munich was serene. Small town after small town, trees and quaint cities. Melissa rode in the car with Marc, observing all the beautiful flowers.

She was surrounded by an oasis of scented, pretty flowers. Simone had them specially ordered and shipped from Africa—they would be used to decorate the cabin and reception hall.

Following the wedding, the reception was in a barn. What a unique idea! It was such an authentic and nature-filled occasion. Many of the guests were dressed in their traditional German clothing. Simone was a beautiful bride, adorned in a classic White dress.

She had planned each element of the wedding to the very last detail. The music was significant in its selection. Simone walked down the aisle with her dad to *Can't Take My Eyes Off Of You* and then added *An Empire State of Mind* to the song list. She concluded the song choice with *Ain't No Mountain High Enough.*

Simone always had a way of letting pictures and music tell her story. The flowers from South Africa draped the tables with elegance. A beautiful Red King Protea circled around teal napkins that Simone had sewn.

The weather even cooperated with her plans. The sky was framed with mountains that were strategically layered with tall trees, showered with different shades of green and brown leaves. It was a perfect picture for a postcard.

Melissa knew God's craftsmanship was at work. The grass was a forest green color that had patches of brown grass, and the sky had an overcast of white and gray clouds. The air had the crisp feel of late fall, with winter peaking around the corner. Autumn had just past its peak with ripeness, beauty and covered with love.

The confluence of German and American culture combined with black culture was on display that day. They all agreed "Love is Love," no matter the color or culture.

Several days after the wedding, Melissa and her family took a train and travelled the countryside of Europe to Vienna. What a lovely ride! The train ride and countryside were everything someone might imagine seeing in a movie. They heard the sound of the train racing over the tracks, and she saw the country towns, with the backdrop of mountains in front of white barns and tall white church steeples.

Bodies of water reflected the sky, and stately trees briskly passed by the windows. In nearby towns, old concrete apartment buildings stood at attention. The ride provided a European history lesson. Soon, they arrived at their destination and enjoyed the culture of a different company.

On the day of her birthday, the day began with a 7 a.m. flight. It was chaotic and confusing, as travel was a bit different overseas than in the states. Though it was early and her family was a bit cranky, she smiled with satisfaction because she knew God was with her.

As her family boarded the plane, they were pleasantly surprised to be upgraded to the 1st and 2nd row. It was a welcome surprise and certainly a pleasant way to travel. As the plane took off, they knew they'd soon would be landing in another country, where Melissa would enjoy the history of culture of many monuments.

Although she had been concerned about the cost of the trip due to her not working, God took care of that challenge. He brought her a travel agent who presented her with an overwhelming great travel package, with a first-class airline seats and amenities. All it took was "mustard seed faith" and that surrendered and trusted in God (plus an extra smile to her loving and supportive husband).

She said it was her gift from God, as once she surrendered and decided to trust, everything then came together at a rate that was unimaginable. She even was able to fly out of her hometown airport, where it seemed ticket prices were usually much higher. The experience of the trip was more than she could have imagined.

Chapter 12

I Will Be with You in the Darkest Times

I have no one else like him who genuinely cares about your welfare. — *Philippians 2:20*

An Untimely Death

It was Friday morning in mid-January and Melissa had awakened early. She was excited and looking forward to taking her mentee to the Historical Museum and having lunch. While in the shower, enjoying the light invigorating warm water running down her body, she mentally prepared for her day. She was listening to the sounds of beautiful gospel music, meditating on the words, smelling an aromatic scented candle, and soaping up with Jo Malone Orange Blossom shower gel.

She was enjoying this time alone with meditation while worshiping God when the telephone rang. She hoped she would not be interrupted until she completed her intimate fellowship with God. However, the ringing persisted for several minutes, with the caller repeatedly calling back.

She eventually realized the caller would not stop calling until she answered. *Who is so desperately trying to reach me?* Reluctantly, she succumbed to the ringing of the phone, exited the shower and answered the call.

It was her niece, Tiffany, frantically shouting that "Joyce is dead!" Was Melissa hearing correctly? Had her 62-year-old sister, Joyce, died? Tiffany repeated, even more loudly, stating, "Joyce is dead!" All Melissa could think was "It can't be." Last week, two days ago, they had talked, and she was fine.

They had talked extensively over the holidays. Her sister had even planned to visit with her and to attend her PhD graduation party as well as the funeral for her mother-in-law.

Joyce told her how proud she and her husband were of Melissa's hard work.

They had planned to celebrate at the graduation party, but at the last minute, they were unable to attend, because her husband was not feeling well. He had been having medical problems that would prevent Joyce from doing many activities. Though Melissa was disappointed, she understood. Melissa never imagined that conversation between her and Joyce would be the last.

After getting off of the telephone, she cancelled her plans with her mentee and prepared to head to Cleveland. She packed a bag and drove her dented damaged car to her hometown. She had no time to think about a rental—her car would have to do.

The car was functional but drafty and whistling from the big dent on the driver's side door from the accident. Still in disbelief about the news from her niece, she completed a drive that normally took three hours in two and a half hours… in winter weather.

The Funeral

She arrived in her hometown to comfort her niece, Spice. Spice and Ericka were her sister, Joyce's daughters, who had a close sibling relationship. Ericka was older and always seemed to be the protector of Spice, from childhood to adulthood. Melissa had always treasured her relationship with her nieces and loved them dearly.

Spice was extremely close to her mom, with whom she spoke multiple times daily. Joyce helped Spice with her son, and she was always present for every school event and activity of her grandson. Melissa could not imagine the impact Joyce's passing would have on Spice and her son. Spice would be devastated for months to come.

While awaiting Ericka's arrival from out of state, Melissa assisted Spice with notifying family and friends, and assisting with her ailing father, who had late-stage Alzheimer's and now would have to move in with Spice until new housing arrangements could be made for him.

Ericka, the elder of the sisters, arrived, and she was in as much shock as they were. At 62, there were no signs signaling Joyce's untimely death. After a day passed, and after speaking with Ericka and Spice, the three began making the funeral arrangements. Melissa centered her thoughts on the scriptre, *God will give you wisdom and answer your prayers — James 1:5.*

She had never felt a greater time to be present for her nieces than during that time of need. There was no time for her personal grieving. Her nieces had lost their mother. She knew the pain that the death of a mother carried, as she had lost her mom just two years ago, and her husband had lost his mother a month earlier.

Maternal grief was difficult, especially since there had been no warning signs. She had to focus on how she could help and comfort her nieces while also assisting them in navigating black family drama, from which no family is exempt. She knew that *Satan comes to steal, kill and destroy — John 10:10.* So she would stay, girded up with prayer and reading the word of God.

In the ensuing days, the three of them were surrounded with angels who comforted them. These were people coming by, sending meals, sending flowers, and driving them about town to take care of much needed business.

Cousin Kaye was right there and said, "I'll do the repast." Melissa was most appreciative. Kaye asked her "to just get the chicken and the place," and she would provide the rest. Kaye decorated the hall, provided sides—i.e. green beans, potato salad, rolls, mac and cheese and desert, and lots of love.

Melissa and her nieces were beyond grateful for the kindness and generosity, but there was so much more to be concerned about other than chicken and a place. There were many other concerns about the future. What would happen with Spice's dad? Who would help with their business matters?

All attention had to shift focus on the issues of the present, not tomorrow. Melissa would think *therefore, do not worry about tomorrow, for tomorrow will worry about itself. Each day has enough trouble of its own — Matthew 6:34.*

Spice and Erica were planning the arrangements for what they wanted for their mother's Home Going service, but at that point, they still did not have a pastor to officiate the funeral services.

Melissa helped with the arrangements, when and where it was appropriate. She knew it was a sacred expression to honor one's mother at her funeral, so she did not want to impose on that task they had undertaken. She made suggestions and pitched in where she felt it was needed and appropriate.

She asked a person to officiate the funeral, but due to prior commitments, he was unable to do it. He had not known her sister, and if he had conducted the services, it would have been a canned, impersonal type of service.

While discussing the death of her sister and giving his condolences, he questioned, "What about *you*?" Melissa thought, *"What about me? What are you thinking?"* She quickly replied, "No, I don't think so."

Nevertheless, he thought it was a great suggestion. Yes, she knew a bit of the word, could speak in front of people and knew and loved her sister. But she had never conducted a eulogy or funeral service, and she did not know how she felt about doing it. Would she be strong enough to do the eulogy?

She lacked the knowledge of the specific and appropriate words that the pastor said at the cemetery. Since she was so uncomfortable with the suggestion, she asked her nieces to check if the funeral home could conduct that part of the services.

While she was certainly willing to support her nieces, she felt uncomfortable about standing in as an officiant. However, after speaking with her nieces and consulting with several

Cleveland pastors, her nieces indicated they wanted Melissa and Cynthia, a childhood friend, to facilitate the services, including the eulogy.

So reluctantly Melissa agreed to honor her nieces' wishes. They wanted to express their love in a non-traditional funeral service for their mother. It would be a love story tribute, with Cynthia being the Mistress of Ceremony, ushering in the focal points of the funeral with scripture, love letters, remarks, and Melissa would do the eulogy.

Now then go, and I, even I, will be with your mouth, and teach you what you are to say — Exodus 4:12. There would be lots of intermingled commentary. What amazed Melissa was how God was present at the funeral and was still answering prayers and using her.

An Unexpected Comment

Melissa was seated in the center of the second row, right behind her nieces and her brother-in-law. She could look directly in the casket and directly at the podium. She sat attentively in a somber mood, waiting there until she delivered the eulogy. At times her head was down, because she was often in a daze.

When Cynthia opened the program for remarks, Melissa didn't know who would feel moved to speak, if anyone. Cousin Brandon stood up as the first to speak. Melissa was thankful that someone would be the first, since often individuals are a bit nervous. With Brandon going first, she was happy.

She was grateful that someone was courageous enough to get up and be first. He commenced to talk about his memories of her sister and a particular story that highlighted how much Joyce smiled. Through the story, Melissa was happy to relive moments of her sister, but she could not help but hear Brandon announce that he had been back from being gone for 12 years.

He repeated the statement a few times, perhaps from nervousness, but Melissa thought, *back from where?*

She knew the answer, but she wondered if others knew. She wondered why he felt the need to make that statement so many times. She guessed that tidbit helped with the flavor of the story. After the funeral, Melissa thanked him for his kind words, for being courageous and being the first to speak.

He simply looked her in the eyes and said, "Girl! I have robbed banks and served time! Speaking in front of crowds is not a problem for me." Melissa reflected for a bit and thought that he made a good point, which put things in perspective.

Being behind bars or speaking for 3 minutes in front of people at a funeral was not a difficult choice—he had a point. Others spoke and brought great memories of her sister. There was quite a bit of humor at the funeral. Joyce would have had it no other way.

The humor did not stop. Next, her older cousin, Dora, came to the podium. Even though the years had passed and she had grown distinguish and wise with her gray hair, Dora always enjoyed engaging in conversation with a story.

As a child Melissa always admired her lively personality and spirited demeanor. Dora enjoyed dancing, laughing and being with the family. She loved a good party. She still enjoyed a hearty laugh and a party. So why did Melissa think that at the podium at the funeral her first words would not be about being at a party in a bar?

Melissa thought as her opening statement was appropriate. It was authentic, Dora recalled pleasant things about Joyce. Her anecdote just happened to be framed around a party and her favorite song about a pony. Yes, Dora brought laughter about Joyce.

Are not all angels ministering spirits sent to serve those who will inherit salvation? — Hebrews 1:14

Next to the podium came a man with a bit of a limp and pimp swag at the same time. *Who is he?* Melissa wondered. He did not look familiar, but Melissa had been gone from the area for a while, so she assumed he must be one of her niece's friends. However, she quickly realized that was not the case.

This gentleman, who calmly yet boldly and confidently walked to the microphone, announced that his name was Pastor Huston, and he did not know the deceased nor the family of the deceased. *Wait! What? Who is he? Why is here?* He said he was a friend of a friend, who was related to the deceased. Melissa wondered how this man found his way in the funeral. *Are people just walking in funerals from off the street?* After some confusion, the room quieted down, with everyone at attention and intrigued by the stranger. People wondered who he was.

He said his friend lived on the east coast in Virginia, and she asked him to attend the funeral on her behalf. She could not be there to support her friend. Melissa wondered, *Do people still do this? Do they drive by to visit a funeral?* Well, she thought it was nice.

Then he said, "Who is Melissa? Please raise your hand." Melissa thought, *This cannot be happening!* She slowly and meekly raised her hand, and he, with a big grin, said that he grew up with her friend from college, and he was there for comfort and condolences. "Your friend could not be here, but she wanted me to bring her condolences and love. I bring them both."

Pastor Huston? *Hmmm.* Wow, that was something else, and it was really happening. All she could think was that *she had not shared with her friend that she had a pastor dilemma.* Melissa had a gamut of emotions going on in her head, but leading the pack was that he was her Ram in the Bush. He was her angel, no matter how he showed up. Yes, he was her angel— even when he did his Q-dog bark at the gravesite, she decided he could conduct the cemetery part of the funeral, and he did.

God Comforts

During her sister's funeral, she felt God was coddling her and saying, *I am here for you; I know your thoughts.* God knew her concerns. It was during that time that Melissa was adjusting to a new routine. This unplanned, newfound freedom led to her having more time available to herself and to getting to know God more deeply.

Yes, she was in a valley, but she was getting used to the terrain of the valley. She had surrendered. During her early mornings, she often praised and worshipped her heavenly Father before starting her day.

She continued to wake up early in the morning, but now she was still, speaking to God, praying to her heavenly Father, listening to her favorite gospel artist and reading multiple quotes of scripture and the word.

That is how she established and started her day. Her routine and relationship with God had changed. She had surrendered and had developed a trusting relationship with her heavenly father. In return, He would communicate with her now in ways where she recognized him more easily. Melissa was at peace and with joy.

Chapter 13

Moving Forward

My dear friends, we are now God's children, but it is not yet clear what we shall become. But we know that when Christ appears, we shall be like him, because we shall see him as he really is. — 1 John 3:2

What's Next?

Once she returned home, she found solace in writing and exploring what God would have her to do. She continued volunteering, working out, dancing, speaking and living. She decided she would not focus on being in the valley, but rather she would have freedom, peace and joy in her present state.

She now lives a more intentional life, a life of self-determination, has a stronger faith in God and sees the possibilities of other opportunities in the midst of difficulties. She exercises, reads her *Bible* more, meditates in scripture and pays attention to God's signs.

She dares to live under the new circumstances of her journey, trusting God, enjoying the moments, being grateful, taking advantage of the adventures, smiling, having a cheerful heart and celebrating who God created her to be.

She turns 55 this year and is grateful that she has developed a closer relationship with God. As she journeys through her life, sometimes with valley moment, she readily *looks to the hills from where her help cometh —Psalm 121:1-2*.

And so often, a wonder or miracle is placed right before her. But rather than live in sorrow, she celebrates the lives and memories of loved ones. She knows all her experiences, good and bad, have provided her with an amazing story. She is thankful for her family and loves fellowshipping with her children and friends.

She continues to submit her research for speaking, visits museums, travels with her husband and explores work opportunities. She speaks at conferences and events about faith and self-determination. She is showcasing her research through the visual eye and lifting the name of Jesus.

Her life has changed dramatically because her relationship with God has changed. She believes that God has shifted her universe to get her attention and to get her in line with His purpose for her life of inspiring others, being bold and courageous, and trusting in his promises. God has shown up many times in her life, with messages of encouragement and assignments to inspire others.

She believes she has been given another opportunity. For the first time, she is able to live her life with freedom, peace and joy. Because of her willingness to listen to God, she has had the ability to travel to places that she has never been to and has dared to dream bigger than she ever has before.

She has seen God use people and do the miraculous in their lives. Melissa knows that *God is not a respecter of person. He shows no favoritism — Romans 2:11.* He can do what he wants for those who believe. God has provided "rams in the bushes" for her. Melissa often says, "Lord open up the heavens and let the rain fall fresh on me. Lead me to where you want me to go. Show me what you would have me to do. Let me align my actions with your will."

Chapter 14

A New Walk

He restoreth my soul; He leadeth me in the paths of righteousness for His name's sake — Psalms 23:3

She now understands that valley moments are for a season and a reason. It is a time of quietness and a time to walk with one's heavenly father. People should approach valley moments in that manner. It's a season for an adjustment. She has learned that time in the valley is a time of reflection.

The feelings of despair, discouragement, sadness or loneliness will not last. The feelings will not be as strong tomorrow as they are today. Each day is a day of getting stronger and closer to one's mountain top. There *will* be a breakthrough! So while in the valley, embrace each step and thrust oneself into the experience of a journey.

Her valley moments have enabled her to appreciate her humanness. She has learned many lessons, been vulnerable, accepted rejection, shown courage, garnered more strength, met new friends, loved more, found peace, trusted God more and found freedom.

She engages in life more by showing up and knowing that God does not make mistakes, but he creates opportunities out of situations that are disguised as problems. She is living her life in a way that she has not done before. She lives intentionally, with a song close to her heart and a new walk.

No matter what the valley is and how devastating, it will require a hope, patience and self-determination that can only come from an intrinsic strength to remember the promises and vows of God. One's faith is crucial. Positive thinking is necessary.

Thus a person must dig and gather every seed of faith and push through heartache and or unanswered question of *How did I end up here?* By believing, someone must surrender to Him and not hold on to things that the person cannot change, but rather strongly grasp and hope for something unbelievable. Be creative, innovative and patient! One must have a belief and an understanding that *what is impossible for man is possible for God — Luke 18:27.*

To travel through one's valley will require a person to see beyond his/her current circumstances and see with a different eye, a clearer eye. This eye is one that requires *a second touch, like when Jesus retouched the blind man a second time — Mark 8:25.* With the first touch, the blind man could only see things that were fuzzy. He could see trees, what was immediately in front of him, but with the second touch, he was able to see clearly.

A person cannot see only the confusion that is in front of that individual. Let that go! One must see beyond that which is immediate, and that means having a clear vision. You must choose to see something other than the confusion, loss, sorrow or fuzzy trees. A person must choose to see the vision beyond the trees and wait for that second touch, and that second touch may be something that is so far-fetched that it is unimaginable.

Being in the valley is not easy, but transformation by God's promises and not being overcome by what one sees is worth the seeming setbacks. **The breakthrough of sunshine to your mountain top will happen... suddenly.**

On Melissa's birthday, while she was with her friend who was undergoing chemo, she received an offer for an outstanding position at a Big 10 institution. The position was something for which she had applied and interviewed for three months prior to her birthday.

She did not anticipate it was where God would have her to be. But the position was carved out just for her. The duties were a culmination of her 25-plus years of experience and education. It was a position where she would utilize her talents, gifts and training. The door that opened would not be closed by man. It was given to her by God.

She was coming out of her valley, physically, but she had come out spiritually long before, for she had surrendered to her God, and she had found freedom, peace and joy. Ironically, two months after starting her new job, her son was accepted at a Big 10 college. He successfully transferred his credits and now attends the college where she works.

A month later, she was selected as a "Woman of Excellence," and she was also asked to give an interview about her faith and self-determination. She believes that life will have trials and tribulations, but one must keep their faith. She feels…

"He lifted me out of the slimy pit, out of the mud and mire; he set my feet on a rock and gave me a firm place to stand... For I live by believing and not by seeing… God in his mercy has given me a new way, I never give up… Though I have been pressed on every side by troubles, I am not crushed. Sometimes perplexed but not driven to despair. I have been knocked down, but I am not destroyed…

I am not abandoned by God."

Psalms 40:2; Hebrews 11:1,2; 2 Corinthians 4:1,2; 2 Corinthians 4:8,9; Deuteronomy 31:6

Author's Note

No one is exempt from valley moments, *consider it pure joy, my brothers and sisters, whenever you face trials of many kinds, because you know that the testing of your faith produces perseverance. Let perseverance finish its work so that you may be mature and complete, not lacking anything — James 1: 2-4* **find freedom, peace and joy!**

For still the vision awaits its appointed time... If it seems slow wait for it; it will not delay... Habakkuk 2:3
Trust in the Lord with all your heart, and do not lean on your own understanding — Proverbs 3:5

References

Collins, P. H. (2002). Black Feminist Thought: Knowledge, Consciousness, and the Politics of Empowerment. Routledge.

Franklin, V. P. (1984). Black Self-Determination: A Cultural History of the Faith of the Fathers. Westport, Conn: L. Hill.

Harris, M. (2010). Black Religion/Womanist Thought/Social Justice: Gifts of Virtue, Alice Walker, and womanist ethics: The disappearance, incarceration, and exile of Argentinean psychoanalysts Palgrave Macmillan US.

Milliman, J., Czaplewski, A.J., & Ferguson, J. (2003). Workplace Spirituality and Employee Work attitudes: An exploratory empirical assessment. Journal of Organizational Change Management, 15(4), 426-447.

www.ingramcontent.com/pod-product-compliance
Lightning Source LLC
Chambersburg PA
CBHW030013110426
42741CB00032B/615